# THE
# S A G A
## OF THE
# VOLSUNGS

### THE NORSE EPIC OF
### SIGURD THE DRAGON SLAYER

Also by Jesse L. Byock
*Feud in the Icelandic Saga*
*Medieval Iceland: Society, Sagas, and Power*

THE COVER:

An eleventh century runestone commemorating the construction of a bridge or a ford at Ramsund, Södermanland, Sweden. The stone shows Sigurd thrusting his sword up into the monster Fafnir. In the center of the carving Sigurd's horse Grani, loaded with treasure, is tied to the tree. In the tree's branches perch the forest birds. To the left, Sigurd is shown roasting Fafnir's heart. Having burned his thumb with the boiling blood, Sigurd sucks on his finger. When the blood gets into his mouth he understands the speech of the birds, warning him of the treachery of the smith. Sigurd kills the smith. The runic inscription reads: "Sigrid, the mother of Alrik, the daughter of Orm, made this bridge for the soul of her husband Holmgr, the father of Sigrid."

# THE
# S A G A
## OF THE
# VOLSUNGS
## THE NORSE EPIC OF
## SIGURD THE DRAGON SLAYER

Introduction and Translation
by
JESSE L. BYOCK

UNIVERSITY OF CALIFORNIA PRESS
BERKELEY    LOS ANGELES    LONDON

University of California Press
Berkeley and Los Angeles, California

University of California Press, Ltd.
London, England

Copyright © 1990 by The Regents of the University of California

Library of Congress Cataloging-in-Publication Data

Völsunga saga. English.
    The Saga of the Volsungs: the Norse Epic of Sigurd the Dragon
Slayer / introduction and translation by Jesse L. Byock.
        p.    cm.
    ISBN 0–520–06683–9 (alk. paper).—ISBN 0–520–06904–8 (pbk.:
alk. paper)
    I. Byock, Jesse L.   II. Title.
PT7287.V7E5   1990
839'.63—dc20                                              89–20313
                                                                CIP

Printed in the United States of America
 4  5  6  7  8  9

To my daughter Ashley
and the fun we had telling the Sigurd
story on a trout fishing trip

# CONTENTS

*Chapter titles with an asterisk have been supplied by the translator; all other titles
are in the original manuscript.

CONTENTS

# Maps

# INTRODUCTION

The unknown Icelandic author who wrote *The Saga of the Volsungs* in the thirteenth century based his prose epic on stories found in far older Norse poetry. His sources, which may have included a lost earlier prose saga, were rich in traditional lore. *The Saga of the Volsungs* recounts runic knowledge, princely jealousies, betrayals, unrequited love, the vengeance of a barbarian queen, greedy schemes of Attila the Hun, and the mythic deeds of the dragon slayer, Sigurd the Volsung. It describes events from the ancient wars among the kings of the Burgundians, Huns, and Goths, treating some of the same legends as the Middle High German epic poem, the *Nibelungenlied*. In both accounts, though in different ways, Sigurd (Siegfried in the German tradition) acquires the Rhinegold and then becomes tragically entangled in a love triangle involving a supernatural woman. In the Norse tradition she is a valkyrie, one of Odin's warrior-maidens.

In Scandinavia, during the centuries after the Middle Ages, knowledge of the Sigurd story never died out among the rural population. Full of supernatural elements, including the schemes of one-eyed Odin, a ring of power, and the sword that was reforged, the tale was kept alive in oral tradition. In the nineteenth century, as the Volsung story was discovered by the growing urban readership, it became widely known throughout Europe. Translated into many languages, it became a primary source for writers of fantasy, and for those interested in oral legends of historical events and the mythic past of northern Europe. The saga deeply influenced William Morris in the nineteenth century and J. R. R. Tolkien in the twentieth. Richard Wagner, in particular, drew heavily upon the Norse Volsung material in composing the Ring cycle. In 1851 he wrote to a friend concerning the saga:

> Already in Dresden I had all imaginable trouble buying a book that no longer was to be found in any of the book shops. At last I found it in the Royal Library. It . . . is called the *Völsunga saga*—translated from Old Norse by H. von der Hagen [1815]. . . . This book I now need for repeated perusal. . . . I want to have the saga again; not in order to imitate it . . . , rather, to recall once again exactly every element that I already previously had conceived from its particular features. [Wagner's use of the Volsung material is discussed later in this Introduction.]

One can only speculate about the origin of the saga's dragon slaying and of other mythic events described in the tale. Many of the saga's historical episodes, however, may be traced to actual events that took place in the fourth and fifth centuries A.D., the period of great folk migrations in Europe. In this time of upheaval, the northern frontier defenses of the Roman Empire collapsed under the pressure of barbarian peoples, as Germanic tribes from northern and central Europe and Hunnish horsemen from Asia invaded what is now France and Germany. A seemingly endless series of skirmishes and wars were fought as tribes attempted to subjugate their enemies and to consolidate newly won territories into kingdoms and empires.

The memory of the migrations became part of the oral heritage of the tribesmen, as epic poems about heroes and their feats spread throughout the continent during succeeding centuries. In the far north legends and songs about Burgundians, Huns, and Goths, as well as new or revised stories about indigenous northern families such as the Volsungs, became an integral part of the cultural lore of Scandinavian societies. The old tales had not died out by the Viking Age (ca. 800–1070), that is, several centuries after the migration period had ended. On the contrary, during this new age of movement in Scandinavia the epic cycles of the earlier migration period seem to have gained in popularity. As Norsemen sailed out from Viking Scandinavia in search of plunder, trade, and land, they carried with them tales of Sigurd and the Volsungs.

One of the places to which the Norsemen carried these epic lays was Iceland, an island discovered by Viking seamen in the ninth century, which soon after its settlement (ca. 870–930) became the major Norse outpost in the North Atlantic. In Iceland, as in the Norse homelands and other overseas settlements, the traditions about Sigurd and the various tribesmen—among them Huns, Goths, and Burgundians—became choice subjects for native poets.

*The Saga of the Volsungs* was written down sometime between 1200 and 1270. Its prose story is based to a large degree on traditional Norse verse called Eddic poetry, a form of mythic or heroic lay which developed before the year 1000 in the common oral folk culture of Old Scandinavia. Eighteen of the Eddic poems in the thirteenth-century *Codex Regius,* the most important manuscript of the *Poetic (or Elder) Edda,* treat aspects of the Volsung legend. (The specific extant poems on which the saga author relied are listed at the end of the book.) This manuscript, which is the only source for many of the Eddic poems, is, however, incomplete. An eight-page lacuna occurs in the middle of the Sigurd cycle, and the stories contained in *The Saga of the Volsungs,* chapters 24–31, are the principal source of information on the narrative contents of these lost pages.

So popular was the subject matter of the saga in the period of oral transmission that, if we are to believe later Icelandic written sources, some of the stories traveled as far as Norse Greenland. Someone in this settlement, founded in 985 by Icelanders led by Erik the Red, may have composed the Eddic poem about Attila (Atli) the Hun called "The Greenlandic Lay of Atli." This poem of heroic tragedy and revenge was later written down and preserved in Iceland.

Written Icelandic material builds on a long oral tradition. By the tenth century the Icelanders had already become renowned as storytellers throughout the northern lands, and Icelandic poets, called skalds, earned their keep in the royal courts of Scandinavia and Anglo-Saxon England. We may assume that, along with many other stories, they told the Sigurd cycle just as German poets told the story of Siegfried. It is noteworthy that about the year 1200, the *Nibelungenlied,* with its poetic version of the Siegfried story, was written, probably in Austria. At approximately the same time or within seven decades, *The Saga of the Volsungs* was compiled in Iceland with far fewer chivalric elements than its German counterpart.

It is not by chance that in Scandinavia so much of the narrative material about the Volsungs was preserved in Iceland. This immigrant society on the fringe of European civilization, like frontier societies in other times and places, preserved old lore as a treasured link with distant homelands. Fortunately for posterity, writing became popular among the Icelanders in the thirteenth century, when interest in old tales was still strong. Almost all the Old Norse narrative material that has survived—whether myth, legend, saga, history, or poetry—is found in Icelandic manuscripts, which form the largest existing vernacular literature of the medieval West. Among the wealth of written material is Snorri Sturluson's *Prose Edda,* a thirteenth-century Icelandic treatise on the art of skaldic poetry and a handbook of mythological lore. The second section of Snorri's three-part prose work contains a short and highly readable summary of the Sigurd cycle which, like the much longer prose rendering of the cycle in *The Saga of the Volsungs,* is based on traditional Eddic poems. Although Snorri and the unknown author of *The Saga of the Volsungs* were treating the same material, there is no indication that the latter was familiar with Snorri's *Prose Edda.*

In the Middle Ages, when most narrative traditions were kept alive in verse, the Icelanders created the saga, a prose narrative form unique in Western medieval culture. Why the Icelanders became so interested in prose is not known, but it is clear that they cultivated their saga form, developing it into a suitable vehicle for long tales of epic quality, one of which is *The Saga of the Volsungs.* At times it seems as if its anonymous author was consciously trying to make history from the mythic and legendary material of his sources. It is also possible that he was drawing upon an earlier prose saga about the Volsungs. He may have been influenced by *The Saga of Thidrek of Berne,* a mid-thirteenth-century Norwegian translation of tales from north and west Germany about King Theodoric the Ostrogoth, a heroic figure from the migration period later called Dietrich of Berne. This saga is a rambling collection of stories about the king, his champions, their ancestors, and several renowned semimythic heroes, including Sigurd.

Along with tales of Sigurd and those of historical peoples and events, *The Saga of the Volsungs* recounts eerie stories whose roots reach back into European prehistory. When Sigurd's father Sigmund is driven from society by his enemy the king of Gautland (in southwestern Sweden), Sigmund finds a companion in his son Sinfjotli. Away from other humans, the two live in an underground dwelling, clothe themselves in wolfskins, and howl like wolves. They roam the forest as beasts of prey, killing any men they come upon. This section of the tale may be interpreted in light of traditions concerning some of Odin's warriors who, according to Snorri Sturluson, behaved like wolves. The description of Sigurd's kinsmen living like werewolves may also shed light on the "wolf-warriors." Helmets and sword scabbards decorated with these strange figures, perhaps werewolves or berserkers, date from the sixth through the eighth century and have been found widely in northern and central Europe. The account of Sigmund and his son Sinfjotli in the forest, and others like it in the saga, reflect the uncertain boundaries between nature and culture and between the world of men and the world of the supernatural. The saga's frequent descriptions of crossings of these borders reveal glimpses not only of fears and dreams but also of long-forgotten beliefs and cultic practices. Not least among these is Sigurd's tasting the blood of the dragon, thereby acquiring the ability to understand the speech of birds. The mixture of arcane knowledge and oral history in the Volsung material proved a potent lure for Norse audiences.

## REPRESENTATIONS OF THE VOLSUNG STORY IN NORSE ART

The story of Sigurd and the lost treasure of the Burgundians was a favorite subject for artists as well as for storytellers in medieval Scandinavia. The many existing wood and stone carvings of scenes from the story testify to its extraordinary popularity in the Viking world, a cultural area that by the year 1000 stretched from Greenland to Scandinavian settlements in Russia (see map 1). The most frequently illustrated scenes are the reforging of the sword Gram, the killing of the dragon Fafnir, the roasting of the dragon's heart, the birds giving Sigurd advice, and Sigurd's horse Grani, often

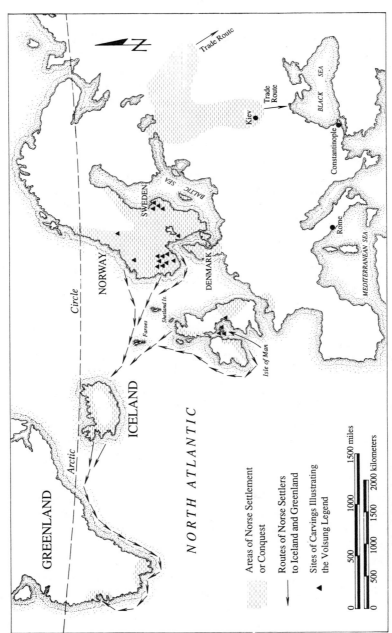

MAP 1. The world of the Vikings (ca. 1000)

loaded with treasure from the hoard. A frequently depicted episode from the second part of the saga shows Sigurd's brother-in-law King Gunnar bound in the snake pit, playing a harp with his toes.

Most extant carvings of the Sigurd legend appear on Christian artifacts such as stone crosses, baptismal fonts, stave church portals, and Christian rune stones. The earliest carvings that clearly portray scenes from the Sigurd legend are found on tenth- and eleventh-century stone crosses from the Isle of Man. Because of its central position in the Irish Sea, with easy access to England, Ireland, Scotland, and Wales, the Isle of Man served as a major Viking base and trade center. It was a meeting place during the Viking Age for Norse and Celtic cultures, including pagan and Christian religions. Baptismal fonts, like the one in the Horum church in Bohuslan, often portray King Gunnar in the snake pit playing the harp with his feet. Farther to the east, in Sweden, a number of clear representations of the Sigurd story include the famous rune stone from Ramsund showing Sigurd slaying the dragon from underneath.

The most numerous Sigurd carvings, however, are found on portals from twelfth- and thirteenth-century Norwegian stave churches. Norway in the Middle Ages had between a thousand and twelve hundred of these sometimes towering wooden structures, many of which survived until the early part of the nineteenth century. Today only about thirty stave churches remain standing. Of the portals that are preserved from churches, many of them demolished in the nineteenth century, three represent biblical scenes; all other carvings portraying human figures are based on the legends of Sigurd and King Gunnar. The portrayal of the legend on church entryways in Norway is particularly intriguing. An Old Norwegian sermon (dated ca. 1200) concerning the consecration of stave churches suggests that for these buildings, as for many other churches, the door symbolically represented a spiritual defense of the interior. Dragon slaying was suitable for representation on church portals and on other Christian carvings because in medieval Christian thought the dragon and the serpent were often connected with Satan. Cast from heaven, Satan is depicted in medieval art as a voracious monster who angrily consumes his victims.

Sigurd crossed the threshold from pagan to Christian hero because of his dragon-slaying characteristics and, perhaps, his association with the Norwegian royal house. Until other warrior-saints became popular in the High Middle Ages, the archangel Saint Michael was the foremost dragon slayer and defender against Satan and chaos. His cult developed early in Scandinavia, and as a dragon slayer he was represented in carvings on church portals in medieval Denmark. In Norway no pre-1200 representations of Michael have been preserved, and there is no mention of carvings of this saint on Norwegian stave church portals. Can the reason for the Norwegian choice of Sigurd over Michael as dragon slayer lie in the politics of the time? Michael was a guardian angel of the Danes, the Baltic Germans, and the Ottonian rulers of the Holy Roman Empire. Since Norway may have regarded him as the symbol of aggressive foreign powers, both lay and ecclesiastic, he would be seen as an inappropriate guardian of Norwegian interests. Sigurd, meanwhile, through the tradition that his daughter Aslaug was married to the legendary ninth-century Viking hero Ragnar Lodbrok ("Hairy Breeches"), was regarded as an ancestor of the Norwegian royal house and thus a suitable champion for Norwegian Christians.

## MYTHS, HEROES, AND SOCIAL REALITIES

*The Saga of the Volsungs* falls into two distinct parts. The first part, ending with Sigurd's arrival among the Burgundians, is studded with mythic motifs, although their religious meaning and their coherence are often lost. Characters in this section include many supernatural beings: gods, giants, a valkyrie, a dwarf, and a dragon. It is difficult to discern historical precedents even for the human characters in this section. By contrast, the second part of the saga takes place in a human world with recognizable social problems. Nearly all the characters in this section may be identified with historical figures.

The first part of the saga is a valuable source of information about Odin, the one-eyed god of war, wisdom, death, and ecstasy. Odin appears here as ancestor and patron of the Volsung line and its scion, the dragon slayer Sigurd. Many of the god's characteristics described in the saga are corroborated by other sources. For example, Odin appears in other Scandinavian and Anglo-Saxon traditions as a progenitor of royal families. He also often bestows gifts on warrior-heroes, a function that he fulfills several times in the saga. It is Odin who first provides the magical sword that Sigurd later inherits from his father Sigmund. Odin also advises Sigurd how to identify the special horse Grani, a descendant of the god's own eight-legged steed Sleipnir.

Sigurd is an Odinic hero, and at crucial moments for Sigurd's ancestors, Odin's intervention assures the continuation of the family that is to produce the monster slayer. Thus when the marriage bed of Sigurd's great-grandfather, King Rerir, is barren, Odin sends Rerir an apple of fertility. The token is carried by a "wish-maiden," one of Odin's supernatural women who flies in the guise of a crow, a carrion bird similar to Odin's ravens. This divine intervention results in the miraculous birth of King Volsung. Later Volsung further reinforces the progenitorial link with the god by marrying the wish maiden who brought the apple that precipitated his own birth. The implied incestuousness of this marriage is echoed later in the saga by the sexual union of Volsung's twin children, Sigmund and Signy. Volsung has an additional connection with fertility cults: his name corresponds to an Old Norse fertility god called Volsi, whom Norwegian peasants represented as a deified horse phallus in *The Tale of Volsi.* This short Christian satire on pagan beliefs probably contains elements of actual pagan ritual. The tale was inserted into *The Saga of Saint Olaf* found in *Flateyjarbók,* a major fourteenth-century Icelandic manuscript named for the island Flatey in western Iceland where the book was found.

Odin, together with the silent god Hoenir and the trickster Loki, sets in motion the events that bring a great treasure from the chthonic world of the dwarves into the world of men. The treasure, which passes through the hands of nearly all classes of beings in the Norse cosmos—dwarves, gods, giants, a dragon, and humans—carries a curse and serves to link the human tragedy of the second part of the saga with the supernatural prehistory of the first part. A particular item in the treasure is a special ring called Andvaranaut, a cursed magical object that even Odin is not able to keep for himself.

What purpose, we may ask, do Sigurd's supernatural advantages and Odin's patronage serve? Although Sigurd has many semidivine attributes, he does not thirst after immortality as do many heroes. The patronage of the highest god and Sigurd's special equipment make him formidable among men but not invincible. The issue of immortality is more clearly drawn in the *Nibelungenlied,* where Siegfried bathes in the blood of the dragon and, like Achilles, becomes invulnerable to weapons except in one part of his body. Furthermore, unlike the exploits of such monster slayers as Beowulf and the heroes of creation epics, Sigurd's dragon slaying and subsequent knowledge do not bring order or safety to the world. On the contrary, his memorable deed has disastrous consequences: almost all persons who come in contact with Sigurd or his family experience tragedy.

Sigurd's susceptibility to the opposing attractions of the real and supernatural worlds is perhaps heightened by the ambivalence of his own nature. Though finally incorporated by marriage into the real world of the Burgundians, he retains certain supernatural abilities, such as the power to assume the shape of others. He uses his otherworldly powers of shape-changing to trick Brynhild by appearing in the guise of his brother-in-law. For reasons that are not explained, Odin distances himself from Sigurd after the monster has been slain. Perhaps Sigurd is no longer of use to the god. It is noteworthy that, after the killing of the dragon, Odin appears only once more in the saga, at the tale's end, when he counsels Jormunrek the Gothic king on how to kill Gudrun's sons.

An overriding theme of tension between marriage and blood bonds runs through the saga. For generation after generation, strife with kin by marriage brings a series of misfortunes upon the Volsungs. Marriage creates new kinship alliances, which are vital for survival in societies like the one pictured in the saga, where there is no effective central order and only a rudimentary judiciary. Many of the saga's major characters are kings or noble retainers, individuals prepared to fight regularly to maintain their status. Even though pledges were exchanged between lord and retainer, the most trustworthy defense lay in the family. Yet villainy often arose from within that social unit, especially in the weak link of the in-law relationship.

In the saga, the Volsungs seldom have dependable blood relations. Sigurd grows up without a father, an element of his upbringing for which the dragon mocks him. The absence of the support that blood relations might supply exacerbates Sigurd's problems with in-laws, who are often untrustworthy. Germanic societies tended to be patrilocal: that is, a man married a woman outside his group and brought her to live with his family instead of their living with hers. Sigurd breaks the usual social pattern after marrying the Burgundian princess Gudrun by settling among his in-laws at Worms. There the protection of both his person and his treasure is dependent upon the goodwill of his wife's Burgundian kinsmen.

The saga makes much of the disturbing fact that Sigurd's brothers-in-law plot against him, even though two of them have increased their obligations to him by establishing blood brotherhood. It is the third Burgundian brother, not bound to the outsider by a ritual blood tie, who carries out the attack on Sigurd. In part the recurring pattern of strife among in-laws comes from the sources available to the saga author. Many of the poems he drew upon for his prose narrative were small tragedies that, like the saga, focused on intrafamily rivalry over treasure and status. Linked together one after the other, the small tragedies weave a larger tale of horror.

## HISTORY AND LEGEND: BURGUNDIANS, HUNS, GOTHS, AND SIGURD THE DRAGON SLAYER

Because verifiable information about the migrations era is limited, the period is a historical snake pit that requires scholars to act much like King Gunnar, who in the saga played the harp with his toes. The writings of Greeks and Romans about their barbarian opponents and neighbors have in modern times come under increasing scrutiny, and the old assumption that tribal names necessarily denote significant or continuing ethnic, cultural (archaeological), or political grouping is questionable. Differing views that often depend on interpretation cannot be proved or disproved by reference to irrefutable fact, since the sources are often uncritical or incomplete and at times are contradictory. For example, four different accounts in ancient writings record the destruction of the Burgundians. It is possible that "Burgundians" becomes a topos in classical sources and in Germanic material, the equivalent of disaster to a family through betrayal. To whatever degree this idea may or may not be valid, connecting the saga and poetic references with historical events is certainly speculative.

The element of speculation is further increased by an awareness of the way in which legends grow. The process of taking root in oral memory tends to obscure their origins, and this observation is true regarding the deadly clash between the Burgundians, led by Gunnar and Hogni, and the Huns under King Atli (Attila, called Etzel in German sources). The most that can be said about Gunnar, for example, is that the historical king of the Burgundians, Gundaharius, is one of the main sources for the fictional King Gunnar; the two are by no means identical. In some instances a legend may develop so fully that its hero shares only a name with the historical figure with whom he is identified. In other instances, legendary and historical events may correspond without any association between the names of the figures involved.

Often characters who lived centuries or decades apart become contemporaries in legend. In *The Saga of the Volsungs,* for instance, Gundaharius (d. 437), Attila (d. 453), and Ermenrichus (king of the Goths, d. 375) are presented as the contemporaries Gunnar, Atli, and Jormunrek. Conflicts between nations or tribes are often reduced to quarrels between families, as witnessed by the way the saga treats the struggle between the Burgundians and the Huns. The absence of evidence that the Icelandic saga audience understood or gave any thought to the ethnic difference between the Huns and the Germanic tribesmen is noteworthy. The oriental origin of Attila is forgotten, and he is treated as one of several competing leaders in the migration period.

If we have come to question classical writings, the writers themselves, especially in the period of the late Roman Empire, seem to be secure in their views: those who mention the Burgundians perceived them as a historical people. The Roman historian Tacitus, writing about the Germanic tribes beyond the Rhine frontier at the end of the first century A.D., unfortunately does not mention the Burgundians, and we have no certain knowledge about their earliest history. In late classical and early medieval sources they are associated with the island of Bornholm in the Baltic Sea. Scholars now generally doubt such a connection, and attempts to demonstrate archeologically a postulated migration from Scandinavia to the mainland in the first century B.C. have been unsuccessful. Nevertheless, a Scandinavian origin for the Burgundians is at least as logical as any other possibility. By the second century A.D. Burgundians are reported to have been living in the area between the Vistula and Oder rivers, in what is today western Poland. Sometime afterward they began their migration westward, arriving in the mid-third century in the region on the upper and middle Main River in southwestern Germany (see map 2).

The next major move of the Burgundians, to the region around Worms, where the saga places them, is better documented. In the unusually severe winter of 406–407 the Rhine froze, making the border indefensible and enabling large numbers of barbarians to cross into Roman territory. Chief among these invaders were the Vandals, who were themselves under pressure from the Huns farther to the east. The Vandals destroyed the previously important Roman garrison town of Worms in the northern part of the upper Rhine Valley before continuing a migration that took them through France and Spain and eventually into North Africa. On the heels of the Vandals other tribes also passed through Worms, but they too had already moved deeper into Gaul when, around 413, the Burgundians crossed the Rhine and first entered the area. By diplomatic means Roman agents detached the newly arrived Burgundians from alliances with other major intruders, and the Burgundians became *foederati* (client-allies) of the Roman Empire. In the fertile region surrounding Worms (some have argued for Koblenz) they established a short-lived kingdom under the aegis of the Romans. Despite the absence of conclusive archaeological evidence, it has long been supposed that the Burgundians established their royal fortress in the old Roman forum in Worms.

The Romans probably hoped that the Burgundians, once settled, would prove to be a bulwark against the incursions of tribes living east of the border. When in the next decades the Burgundians tried to expand northward into neighboring Roman territory, they incurred the wrath of Aetius, the last great Roman general in Gaul. Aetius knew the barbarian peoples well. He had once been a hostage of the Huns and often enlisted these horsemen as his allies. Relying on a Hunnish mercenary army, Aetius, then the effective leader of the Western Empire, attacked the Burgundians in 436 and completely routed them. The Burgundians, it is said, lost their king Gundaharius, his whole family, and 20,000 men. After the Huns

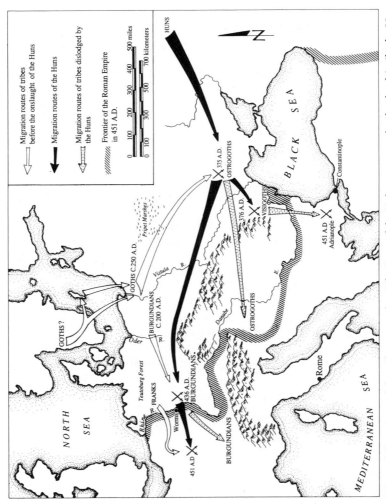

MAP 2. Migrations of the tribes central to *The Saga of the Volsungs* up to the death of Attila the Hun

Migration routes of tribes before the onslaught of the Huns

Migration routes of the Huns

Migration routes of tribes dislodged by the Huns

Frontier of the Roman Empire in 451 A.D.

0 100 200 300 400 500 miles
0 100 300 500 700 kilometers

N

HUNS

GOTHS C.250 A.D.

Pripet Marshes

Vistula R.

BURGUNDIANS C.200 A.D.

GOTHS ?

Oder R.

Teutoburg Forest

FRANKS

Rhine R.

Worms

436 A.D. BURGUNDIANS

451 A.D.

BURGUNDIANS

Danube

375 A.D. OSTROGOTHS

376 A.D.

OSTROGOTHS

VISIGOTHS

451 A.D. Adrianople

Constantinople

BLACK SEA

NORTH SEA

Rome

MEDITERRANEAN SEA

withdrew from the region around Worms, the area was occupied by the Alemanni, another Germanic tribe, who in turn were conquered by the Franks in the late fifth century.

But the Burgundians did not disappear from history. Under the protection of the victorious Aetius, those who survived the battle migrated south to the region near Lake Geneva. In less than two decades the Burgundians had surprisingly regained enough strength to resume their fight against the Huns. In 451, under the generalship of Aetius, they joined with the Franks, the Visigoths, and the Gallo-Romans to repel an invasion of Gaul by Attila. The victorious alliance, however, soon fell apart. The Burgundians turned on the Gallo-Romans and, by defeating them, quickly became a major power within the crumbling empire. By the latter part of the fifth century they had extended their power over most of eastern Gaul and had established their capital at Lyon. The surrounding region came to be called Burgundy, a name it has kept. The Burgundians, however, were unable to maintain their independence. A series of conflicts with the Franks and the Goths sapped their strength, and in 534 what was left of their kingdom was annexed by the Franks. Thereafter the Burgundians were absorbed into Frankish society, eventually losing their ethnic identity.

The Huns were pastoral nomads who originated in the Altai Mountains of central Asia. Because no written record of their native language has survived, we can only guess at the nature of Hunnish languages from names recorded in other peoples' writings. Probably a substantial group of Hunnish peoples spoke some form of Turkic, a subfamily of the Altaic languages. Little definitive information about the Huns' early history is available, although it has long been supposed that they were related to the Hsiung-nu, against whom the Chinese erected the Great Wall. Until the time of Attila in the fifth century, when rudimentary forms of statehood began to take shape, the Huns were chiefly a loose association of different tribes. They were skillful horsemen who fought as mounted archers. The accuracy of their compound bows and their reputation for cruelty inspired fear among enemies.

One such enemy was the Ostrogoths, a people represented in the saga by their king Jormunrek. In the fourth century the Ostrogoths ruled a vast empire north of the Black Sea, stretching across the grasslands of Russia from the Don River to the Dniester and extending from the Crimea to the Pripet marshes. The earliest history of the Goths is shrouded in obscurity, but they almost certainly originated in southern Scandinavia and migrated across the Baltic in the first century A.D., probably giving their name to the Baltic island of Gotland. By the third century the Goths were inhabiting a region near the Vistula, in present-day Poland, before migrating southeast.

By the fourth century the Goths had split into two major groups, the Visigoths, living in present-day Rumania, and the Ostrogoths. How the Ostrogoths acquired their empire and came to dominate the many peoples it included remains a mystery. The Huns fell upon and destroyed the Ostrogothic empire when, around 375, they suddenly invaded the steppes of present-day Russia. Continuing on the offensive, they advanced into central Europe and enslaved the tribes in their path. In 376 they overwhelmed the Visigoths, whose remnants then sought safety within the borders of the Roman Empire. After that victory the Huns settled down on the Hungarian plain, having in three short years wiped out a century-long Gothic expansion.

After destroying the Visigoths, the Huns remained quiet for half a century, but about 430 they were again on the move. It was at this time that the army of Hunnish mercenaries, acting under the orders of Aetius, crushed the Burgundians. At approximately the same time, the Huns, in a series of similar but unconnected raids on other Germanic tribesmen, Romans, and eastern peoples, expanded their own empire until it reached from Europe to the Persian and perhaps even to the Chinese frontier. Beginning in 434, Attila and his brother Bleda ruled the empire jointly. In 445, after murdering his brother, Attila became the sole ruler. His apparently weak control over the eastern part of the empire, however, diminished his ability to acquire sufficient reinforcements of Hunnish warriors and trained horses.

At the heart of the Hunnish empire was its capital, the "Ring," a circular city of tents, wooden palaces, and wagons, at whose center stood Attila's royal residence. Attila's court was a meeting place for hostages, retainers, and warriors from the various subject tribes. Large contingents of the latter were incorporated into the Hunnish armies, whose military organization was modified in Attila's time to reflect the growing importance of units of armored warriors often drawn from the conquered peoples. Poems such as the Anglo-Saxon "Waldere" and parts of the different Sigurd/Siegfried traditions show traces of what most certainly was a series of heroic cycles about Attila's court and the champions of the period.

After Attila's death in 453, his numerous quarreling sons divided the empire into separate dominions. In 454 an alliance of subjected tribes revolted and inflicted a crushing defeat upon their masters. The Goths remained for the most part neutral in this battle, but over the next decade they too fought a series of mostly successful engagements against the Huns. These reversals reduced the Huns to insignificance, and after the mid-sixth century they are no longer mentioned in the sources. Because of the temporary nature of their buildings and towns, no major archaeological trace of the Hunnish empire has been found. The modern Hungarians are not descended from this group but stem from a later migration of the distantly related Magyars.

What is the connection between the historical Huns, Burgundians, and Goths and the characters who play prominent roles in *The Saga of the Volsungs*? The answer is clouded by time. Obviously Atli, king of the Huns in the saga, is based on Attila, and Gunnar represents Gundaharius, the ill-fated Burgundian king. Without doubt the later Burgundians, even under the Franks, retained knowledge of their ancestors. A sixth-century law code names Gibica, Gundaharius, and Gislaharius as early Burgundian rulers. Gibica corresponds to Gjuki, the father of Gunnar; Gundaharius, to Gunnar; and Gislaharius, to Giselher, who appears in the *Nibelungenlied* as one of the kings jointly ruling Burgundy. Atli's betrayal of Gunnar and Hogni in the saga reflects the historical destruction of Gundaharius's kingdom by the Hunnish mercenary army.

The saga's account, however, is far from historically accurate. Among the many discrepancies is the absence of Aetius, the Roman general who commanded the Hunnish mercenaries. Furthermore, the political reasons for the war are lost; events are portrayed as springing from intrafamily feuds, motivated by greed and jealousy among blood relations and in-laws. A major chronological difference is that the historical Attila did not participate in the war against the Burgundians in 436; at that time he was on the middle

Danube negotiating with the Romans. It is not difficult to understand, however, that a storyteller would want to embellish his tale with a character as intriguing as Attila.

The Hunnish king's association with the Burgundians was perhaps an early step in the development of the legend. Certainly the connection of Attila with wealth is well founded. Vast quantities of gold and valuables flowed into his coffers, and large numbers of slaves became his property. As his treasure grew, so did his greed. In 443 the Eastern Roman emperor Theodosius bought peace from Attila at the price of 432,000 solidi, about two tons of gold. Payments of this magnitude brought wealth to the subject tribes serving Attila, enabling large quantities of precious metals to circulate through the northern lands, including Scandinavia. Such exorbitant tributes, along with booty and payments acquired by other tribesmen, provided material for flamboyant jewelry and ornaments.

The saga's account of King Atli's death at a woman's hand also has a foundation in history. The earliest and most reliable report of Attila's death was written by the Greek historian Priscus, who had visited the Huns as a member of a diplomatic mission a few years before Attila died. Priscus's work survives only in fragments, but he is cited at length by the sixth-century Gothic historian Jordanes in his *History of the Goths*:

> He [Attila] near the time of his death, as the historian Priscus tells, married a very beautiful girl named Ildico, after countless other wives, as was the custom of his people. At his wedding he overindulged in gaiety and lay down on his back, heavy with wine and sleep. A gush of blood, which normally would have run down out of his nose, was hindered from its usual channels; it flowed on a fatal course into his throat and killed him. Thus drunkenness brought a scandalous end to a king famed in battle. On the next day, when a good portion of the day had passed, the king's servants suspected something tragic and, after a great clamor, smashed down the doors. They discovered Attila dead without any wounds. His death was caused by an effusive nosebleed, and the girl, her head hanging low, cried under her veil.

Jordanes, who makes an effort to establish the accidental nature of Attila's death, may have been aware of other versions of the story in which Ildico kills Attila, since a contemporary chronicle says that Attila died at the hands of a woman. The woman involved was evidently Germanic; Ildico seems to be a diminutive of the female proper name Hild, which in the form of the suffix -*hild* is a common element in other Germanic female names. For example, the woman in the *Nibelungenlied* who plays the role similar to Gudrun's in *The Saga of the Volsungs* is named Kriemhild.

The saga's Gothic King Jormunrek, like Gunnar and Atli, is based on a historical figure known to the Romans as Ermenrichus, who in the fourth century ruled the vast Ostrogothic empire on the steppes. The contemporary Roman historian Ammianus Marcellinus, in his *History,* claims that Ermenrichus killed himself rather than contend with attacks by the Huns:

> Accompanied by their allies, the Huns burst with a sudden attack into the wide districts of Ermenrichus. Ermenrichus, a very warlike king who terrified nearby peoples because of his many boldly executed deeds, was hit hard by the force of this sudden attack. For a long time, however, he tried to remain strong and resolute. Nevertheless, rumor spread, exaggerating the looming disasters, and he settled his fear of these major crises by his voluntary death.

By the sixth century the legend of Ermenrichus had developed beyond these sparse facts into a recognizable version of the story told in *The Saga of the Volsungs.* Among other new details Jordanes, in his *History of the Goths,* tells of a woman named Sunilda, wife of a leader of a people subject to the Goths. Jordanes mentions the vengeance of her brothers Sarus and Ammius and Hermanaric's death in old age:

> Hermanaric, king of the Goths, as we have reported above, was conqueror of many tribes. Nevertheless, while he was apprehending the approach of the Huns, the treacherous tribe of the Rosomoni, who among others then owed him allegiance, seized the opportunity to turn on him. The king, shaken with rage, ordered a certain chieftain's wife of the above-mentioned

tribe named Sunhilda to be bound to wild horses on account of her husband's treachery. She was then torn asunder by the horses running at full gallop in opposite directions. After this killing, her brothers Sarus and Ammius avenged her death by thrusting a sword into Hermanaric's side. Stricken by his wound, Hermanaric lived out a sickly existence with an enfeebled body. Balamber, king of the Huns, made use of this illness and moved his battle-ready men into the territory of the Ostrogoths, from whom the Visigoths had already separated because of some disagreement between them. Meanwhile Hermanaric, unable to bear the pain of his wound and the distress of the Hunnish invasion, died full of days at the age of 110. Because of his death the Huns prevailed over those Goths who, as we have said, settled in the eastern region and are called Ostrogoths.

Jordanes's story appears, in part, historically accurate: it presents a reasonable chronology and with seeming correctness identifies the peoples involved. At the same time we can see the elements that are to be more fully developed in later legend. Sunilda is manifestly the prototype of Svanhild, Sigurd and Gudrun's daughter, who in the saga is killed by Jormunrek. Likewise the correspondences with Svanhild's brothers Sorli (Sarus) and Hamdir (Ammius) are reasonably clear. Although we will never know precisely what source Jordanes used for this story, it is tempting to postulate that he relied on a now lost heroic lay.

In the centuries that followed, the tale passed more thoroughly from history into legend. Spreading widely, it was known in some form in Anglo-Saxon England, where the tragedy of Ermenrichus (Eormanric) is one of the many referred to in the moving Anglo-Saxon lament *Deor*:

We've heard of the she-wolf's heart
of Eormanric; he ruled the folk
of the Goths' kingdom. That was a
cruel king!
Many men sat bound in sorrow,
expecting woe; often they wished
that the kingdom be overcome.

One can only guess when and how Sigurd became connected with the other legendary elements of the story. Earlier sources yield some evidence that Sigurd may not originally have been the Volsung who slew the dragon. In the Anglo-Saxon epic poem *Beowulf*, the dragon slaying is attributed not to Sigurd, who goes unmentioned, but to Sigemund Waelsing (Volsung), the Anglo-Saxon equivalent of Sigurd's father Sigmund. The poem also mentions Sigemund's nephew Fitela whose name corresponds to the Scandinavian Sinfjotli, who is Sigmund's son by his sister and hence also his nephew:

He told all that he had heard
of the deeds of valor, far voyages
and unknown struggles of Sigemund Waelsing,
feuds and foul deeds; Fitela alone,
and no other men, knew of this,
from when Sigemund chose to speak of the deeds
uncle to nephew, as they ever in battle
were comrades in arms, each to the other—
they killed great numbers of the giant race,
slew them with swords. No scant glory
developed for Sigemund after his death
because the brave warrior killed the serpent
guardian of the hoard.

          Under the gray stone
the prince's [Waels's] son alone performed
a fierce deed—Fitela was not with him.
Even so, it happened that his sword hewed
the ornate serpent; the noble weapon
drove into the wall as the dragon died.
With valor the warrior won the ring hoard,
so that he might enjoy it at his own desire;
The son of Waels loaded his watercraft,
bore bright treasures to the ship's bosom.
The serpent's own fires melted its flesh.

In this Anglo-Saxon version of the story Fitela is described only as Sigemund's nephew, whereas in the Icelandic saga Sinfjotli is both son and nephew to Sigmund. The motif of incest in *The Saga*

*of the Volsungs,* so important to the understanding of the relationship between Sigmund and Sinfjotli as father and son, may be a late
addition to the legend. *Beowulf* refers to the progenitor of the race
of heroes as Waels. In Scandinavia the name of Sigmund's father
was the unusual compound, Volsung, possibly formed when the
patronymic suffix *-ung* (present in the Anglo-Saxon form *Waelsing,*
"Son of Waels") was interpreted as an integral part of the name.

Sigmund appears to be the original dragon slayer, and Sigurd's
filial connection with the old hero is probably an expansion of the
legend. This hypothesis gains additional credence through the absence of Sigurd's name from "The Lay of Eirik," one of the earliest
Scandinavian poems referring to the Volsungs. The lay is a memorial poem for Eirik Bloodaxe, king of Norway and of Viking York.
Composed after the death of this Norse prince in A.D. 954, the
poem has Odin call Sigmund and Sinfjotli to greet Eirik on his arrival in Valhalla, Odin's hall for slain warriors:

> Sigmund and Sinfjotli: Rise up with speed
>     and go to greet the warrior:
> Invite him in, if it be Eirik;
>     I await his arrival.

Who, then, was Sigurd originally? To this difficult question we
will probably never have a definitive answer. Certainly Sigurd was
already a character of myth and legend when he was joined to the
Volsungs. He may even have some basis in history, and in this re-
gard two figures in particular have received attention. One is Arminius, a leader in the first century A.D. of the Cherusci, a Germanic
tribe; the other is the sixth-century Frankish King Sigibert. In both
instances the connection is highly conjectural.

In A.D. 9, in the Teutoburg Forest in northern Germany, Arminius lured the attacking Romans, led by Quintilius Varus, into
a trap and wiped out three Roman legions. For years preceding this
defeat the Roman Empire had been engaging in a costly but gradu-
ally successful conquest of Germania, and the three legions were
the major part of Rome's mobile forces in the West. The Roman
historian Suetonius reports that everyone on the Roman side was
massacred—the legionnaires and the officers, the commander, the
complete staff, and the auxiliary forces. So unsettling was the defeat

that when the news reached Rome, the emperor Augustus commanded that the city be patrolled at night to prevent an uprising. For months afterward Augustus suffered deep despair. He left his beard and hair uncut and, often striking his head against the door to his chamber, he would call out, "Varus, give me back my legions!"

The loss of his legions forced Augustus to abandon the hope of conquering Germania permanently. He fixed the border protecting Gaul and the already conquered south German provinces a short distance east of the Rhine. With small adjustments, the frontier between the Romans and the northern barbarians remained fixed for the next four centuries. The border posts finally fell before the migrating tribes in the early fifth century, or about the time of the clash between the Huns and the Burgundians.

For the Romans, the Varus episode, although grievous, was ultimately of less importance than the much larger conflict on the Danube border and the twin-frontier problem (Rhine-Danube) thereafter. Nevertheless, the Romans showed considerable interest in Arminius. Velleius Paterculus, a contemporary first-century writer, describes this barbarian leader (in his synopsis of Roman history) as "a young man of noble descent . . . , valorous and astute, with talents exceeding those of common barbarians. His name was Arminius, the son of Sigimerus, chief of the tribe, and he showed the fire in his soul, by his countenance, and in his eyes." If somewhat of a passing curiosity to the Romans, the Cheruscan leader remained a hero among the barbarians on the northern frontier. The Roman historian Tacitus reports (in his *Annals*) that unwritten songs and lays of Arminius were sung by tribesmen a century after his death.

The arguments for connecting Sigurd with Arminius stress in particular the genealogy of the war leader, most of whose male relatives bore names with the initial element *seg-* or *segi-* (victory), equivalent to Old Norse *sig-*. If Arminius was a Roman name or a Latinized Germanic title, this leader would probably also have had a native name beginning with *seg-*, as alliterating names were a common feature in Germanic families. Furthermore, the *-elda* element in the name of Arminius's wife is similar to the *-hild* element in the names of women connected with Sigurd in later versions.

However appealing this evidence, it should be remembered that these characteristics of nomenclature were common and may well be coincidental.

The Greek geographer Strabo gives more information about Arminius's family. In his geography from the first century A.D. Strabo describes the triumphal procession in Rome in A.D. 17 accorded to Germanicus, a member of the imperial family, who avenged Varus's defeat:

> But they [the tribesmen] all paid the price and gave the young Germanicus a victory celebration, in which their most distinguished men and women were led captive— namely, Segimundus, son of Segestes and leader of the Cherusci, and his sister Thusnelda, wife of Arminius. . . . But Segestes, the father-in-law of Arminius, set himself against the purpose of Arminius from the very beginning and, seizing an opportune time, deserted him; and he was present, and honored, at the triumph over those dear to him.

Strabo's account thus suggests that Arminius, like Sigurd, was betrayed by in-laws.

Other elements in the theory connecting Arminius with Sigurd (Siegfried) are even more hypothetical. Some scholars have suggested a linkage between Sigurd and Arminius on the basis of associated animal imagery, interpreting among other things Sigurd's dragon as a symbolic representation of the dragon banners of the legions destroyed by Arminius. As fascinating as such conjectures may be, the basic fact remains that beyond the general motif of kin strife, the connection is just a supposition and a highly speculative one at that. Little actual correspondence exists between the life of Arminius, as described by Roman historians, and Sigurd's legendary adventures.

A second possibility for the historical origin of Sigurd is the Frankish King Sigibert (A.D. 535–575). As the Merovingian king of Metz, Sigibert ruled a territory that included much of what is today northeastern France, Belgium, and the region on the upper Rhine where the Burgundians lived before their destruction by the Huns in 437. Among Sigibert's subjects were many Burgundians. Sigibert's wife Brunhilda (d. 613) may be loosely identified with Brynhild in the saga. The marriage of Sigibert to this Visigothic princess is reported by the sixth-century Gallo-Roman bishop Gregory of Tours in his *History of the Franks*:

> When King Sigibert saw that his brothers were taking wives who were unworthy of them, even debasing themselves to the point of marrying their female slaves, he dispatched an embassy to Spain with abundant gifts for Brunhilda, daughter of King Athanagild. . . . Her father, not refusing him, sent her to the king with a large dowry. Sigibert assembled the elders and prepared a feast, taking Brunhilda with great joy and delight as wife.

Somewhat like Sigurd, Sigibert was destroyed by strife within his family. The Frankish king was murdered by the mistress of his brother. Brunhilda's subsequent attempts to take revenge within the royal family seriously weakened the Merovingian kingdom, just as Brynhild's revenge in the saga contributes to the fall of the Burgundians. Sigibert's story, as well as Arminius's, bears some resemblance to Sigurd's, but attempting to identify the dragon slayer with either of these two historical figures is not fully convincing. The similarities center mostly on common aspects of the Germanic naming practices and a social milieu where kin strife was frequent.

No one can say exactly when the process of combining the different historical, legendary, and mythic elements into a Volsung cycle began, but it was probably at an early date. By the ninth century the legends of the Gothic Jormunrek and those of the destruction of the Burgundians had already been linked in Scandinavia, where the ninth-century "Lay of Ragnar" by the poet Bragi the Old treats both subjects. Bragi's poem describes a shield on which a picture of the maiming of Jormunrek was either painted or carved and refers to the brothers Hamdir and Sorli from the Gothic section of the saga as "kinsmen of Gjuki," the Burgundian father of King Gunnar.

The "Lay of Ragnar" has other connections with the Volsung legend. The thirteenth-century Icelandic writer Snorri Sturluson identifies the central figure of the lay, whose gift inspired the poem in his honor, with Ragnar Hairy Breeches, a supposed ancestor of the Ynglings, Norway's royal family. Ragnar's son-in-law relationship to Sigurd through his marriage to Sigurd's daughter Aslaug (mentioned earlier in connection with stave church carvings) is reflected in the sequence of texts in the vellum manuscript: *The Saga of the Volsungs* immediately precedes *The Saga of Ragnar Lodbrok*. Ragnar's saga, in turn, is followed by *Krákumál* (Lay of the Raven), Ragnar's death poem, in which Ragnar, thrown into the snake pit by the Anglo-Saxon King Ella, boasts that he will die laughing. The Volsung and Ragnar stories are further linked by internal textual references. It is likely that the *The Saga of the Volsungs* was purposely set first in the manuscript to serve as a prelude to the Ragnar material. The opening section of *Ragnar's saga* may originally have been the ending of *The Saga of the Volsungs*. Just where the division between these two sagas occurs in the manuscript is unclear. Together these narratives chronicle the ancestry of the Ynglings—the legendary line (through Sigurd and Ragnar) and the divine one (through Odin). Such links to Odin, or Wotan, were common among northern dynasties; by tracing their ancestry through Sigurd, later Norwegian kings availed themselves of one of the greatest heroes in northern lore. In so doing, they probably helped to preserve the story for us.

## RICHARD WAGNER AND THE SAGA OF THE VOLSUNGS

Knowledge of *The Saga of the Volsungs* is of special value to Richard Wagner admirers, since the Norse material it contains was a primary source for the composer's cycle of music dramas, the *Ring of the Nibelung*. This nineteenth-century version of the Volsung-Nibelung legend is probably the one best known to the modern reader. As he had earlier depicted the courtly world and its ethic in great detail in *Tannhäuser* and *Lohengrin,* Wagner, in composing the Ring cycle, made less use than is normally assumed of the version of the story found in the South German *Nibelungenlied,* which is essentially a courtly epic. Instead he turned to the more pagan material and attitudes that he found in the Scandinavian sources, especially in Eddic poetry and in *The Saga of the Volsungs.* He explored this mythic world in the Ring cycle as a way of expressing his reflections on his own period and countrymen, intending the *Ring* to be a commentary on the industrial and political revolutions of the nineteenth century. Wagner himself had revolutionary yearnings; he was exiled for his participation in the revolution of 1848.

Not only was Wagner directly inspired by his own reading of *The Saga of the Volsungs* in H. von der Hagen's 1815 German translation, but the composer was also influenced by the treatment of the saga in Wilhelm Grimm's *Deutscher Heldensage.* Wagner appears to have been especially struck by Grimm's interpretation of the sibling marriage in the Norse material, and reading Grimm helped Wagner to form his views about the central importance of *The Saga of the Volsungs* and Eddic poetry. In adapting the Norse material to his own uses, as elsewhere in writing his librettos, Wagner took many liberties with his medieval sources, abridging, changing, condensing, and combining them freely and imaginatively. The dwarf Alberich, in the opening scene of the *Rhinegold,* the prelude to the cycle, is taken from the *Nibelungenlied,* where he is the treasurer of the Nibelung dynasty. The setting in watery depths comes from the Scandinavian tradition and is reflected in the account of the dragon Fafnir found in the saga and in Eddic poetry. The Rhine maidens are borrowed from German folklore. The company of gods and the story of the establishment of Walhalla (Valhalla) were freely adapted by Wagner from the *Prose Edda* of the thirteenth-century Icelander, Snorri Sturluson.

In the *Valkyrie,* the first of the music dramas that form the main body of the cycle, Wagner relied heavily on the version of the legends found in *The Saga of the Volsungs.* Unlike the music drama, the saga meanders through many generations of Volsungs before reaching Sigurd. In the saga, Sigurd's half brother Sinfjotli is of incestuous birth; Wagner transfers this motif, and the dramatic story that surrounds it, to his principal hero, Siegfried (Sigurd). The wisdom imparted to the hero by the valkyrie Brünnhilde (the Norse Brynhild), whom Wagner makes a daughter of Wotan, is an important element in Siegfried's maturation process and one that is most fully described in the Norse material. The fourth and final music drama, the *Twilight of the Gods,* reflects Wagner's familiarity with the plot structure of the *Nibelungenlied.* In this section of the cycle, the role of the villain Hagen (Hogni in the saga) comes principally from the *Nibelungenlied*, as does the sequence in which Siegfried is killed.

The portrayal of the father of the gods illustrates better than anything else the difference between Wagner's version and his sources. The intervention of Odin (Wotan) is more sporadic and less purposeful in the saga than in Wagner's drama. In the *Ring*, the god's actions are motivated by an overriding aim, to regain possession of the magical ring and thus to reassert control over the world. Wotan's deliberate plotting to produce a hero who would regain for him the lost ring and the golden hoard can be seen as a critique of the acquisitiveness of the Industrial Age. Wagner added the dimension of political power to the qualities of the ring. In the Scandinavian sources magic rings possess the power to generate wealth and they carry curses, but Wagner's ring also grants its bearer the power to rule the world. The source for this quality seems to have been a relatively insignificant line from the *Nibelungenlied*, which says that the Nibelung treasure included a tiny golden wand that could make its possessor the lord of all mankind.

In *Siegfried*, Wagner followed the Norse tradition most closely. Wagnerites will quickly recognize the saga's version of the hero's youth, the dragon slaying, the roasting of the monster's heart, and the singing birds that lead him to the sleeping heroine. The mythical pagan world of the saga comes vividly alive in this part of the cycle, although the romantic ideals of the nineteenth century repeatedly dominate Wagner's presentation. At times we can perceive the dramatic reasons for Wagner's changes. Whereas Sigurd in *The Saga of the Volsungs* is treacherously killed in bed, Wagner followed the German version which has the hero die in a splendid forest setting, providing the composer with an opportunity to have his music reflect forest and mountain scenes. Once the hero is dead, however, Wagner returns to the version found in the saga for Brünnhilde's final immolation by fire, and he ends the entire cycle of music dramas in a burst of pagan glory.

Reshaping his Norse sources, Wagner united two stories, unconnected in their Norse forms: the tale of Sigurd and the account of *Ragnarök*, the downfall of the Norse gods. In Wagner's version, the flames of Siegfried's funeral pyre rise to ignite Valhalla, bringing about the twilight of the gods. Wagner's outlook is strongly conditioned by *Völuspá*, a powerful Eddic poem that presents all of cosmic history as inevitably leading to the cataclysmic doom of *Ragnarök*. In *Völuspá*, Odin calls up from her grave a dead giantess to prophesy for him the fate of the gods; this scene was probably a model for Wotan's confrontation with the earth goddess, Erda, in the *Ring*. Although now generally translated as "the fate of the gods," the word *Ragnarök* was earlier interpreted by scholars to mean "the twilight of the gods." Wagner translated this into German as *Götterdämmerung*.

*The Saga of the Volsungs* says that its hero's "name is known in all tongues north of the Greek Ocean, and so it must remain while the world endures." Wagner's Ring cycle has helped to make this thirteenth-century statement true.

# NOTE ON THE TRANSLATION

This translation is based on a single vellum manuscript, Ny kgl. Saml. 1824b 4$^{\text{to}}$, which alone among medieval Icelandic writings preserves *The Saga of the Volsungs* (*Völsunga saga*). This same manuscript also contains *The Saga of Ragnar Lodbrok* (*Ragnars saga loðbrókar*) and Ragnar's death song, *Krákumál*. The manuscript dates to approximately A.D. 1400, although the texts it includes are copies of much older originals. *The Saga of the Volsungs* was first written down no later than 1260–1270, though perhaps as early as 1200. Sent from Iceland to Denmark in the sixteenth century, the manuscript is now in the Royal Library in Copenhagen. *The Saga of the Volsungs* is also found in twenty-one paper manuscripts, dating from the seventeenth through the nineteenth centuries. All these paper copies derive directly or indirectly from the unique vellum manuscript, which is accessible in a series of photographs taken in Copenhagen by Arni Mann Nielsen and in Magnus Olsen's excellent diplomatic edition, *Völsunga saga ok Ragnars saga loðbrókar* (Copenhagen, 1906–1908). As the quality of the medieval manuscript has deteriorated since the early twentieth century, a number of passages, which were legible in Olsen's day, can no longer be read.

The saga has been translated into English four times previously: William Morris and Eiríkur Magnússon (London, 1870); Margaret Schlauch (New York, 1930); R. G. Finch (London, 1965); and George K. Anderson (Newark, Del., 1982). Although frequently disagreeing with their interpretations of the text, I have found all four works useful in the preparation of this translation. I have also consulted Örnólfur Thorsson's excellent modern Icelandic edition (Reykjavík, 1985).

The chapter headings found in the vellum manuscript are at times inaccurate or inappropriate to the content of the chapters. I have, nevertheless, reproduced them as they are found in the medieval text. Where chapter headings are lacking in the manuscript, I have supplied my own and marked them with asterisks.

The spelling of proper names and special terms in the text has been anglicized, usually by omitting the Old Norse inflectional endings and replacing non-English letters with their closest equivalents. I do not strive for complete consistency, especially when a name is familiar to English speakers in another form; thus, I use *Valhalla* rather than *Valholl*. My goal throughout has been to produce an accurate, readable translation of an important medieval text.

# THE
# SAGA
## OF THE
# VOLSUNGS
## THE NORSE EPIC OF
## SIGURD THE DRAGON SLAYER

ODIN GUIDES SIGI
     FROM THE OTHERWORLD*

Here we begin by telling of a man who was named Sigi, and it was
said that he was the son of Odin.[1] Another man, called Skadi, is
introduced into the saga; he was powerful and imposing. Sigi, however, was the more important of the two and was of better stock,
according to what was said in those days. Skadi owned a thrall
called Bredi who should be mentioned in the account of these
events. Bredi was well informed in the things he had to do. He was
equal in skills and accomplishments to those who were thought
more worthy, and he was better than some.

Now there is this to be told: Sigi once went hunting with the
thrall, and they hunted all day until evening. When they compared
their kills in the evening, Bredi's was larger and better than Sigi's,
which greatly displeased Sigi.[2] He said he wondered that a thrall
should outdo him in hunting. For this reason he attacked and killed
Bredi and then disposed of the corpse by burying it in a snowdrift.

That evening Sigi went home and said that Bredi had ridden
away from him into the forest: "He was soon out of my sight, and
I do not know what became of him." Skadi doubted Sigi's story.
He guessed that there was likely to be deception on Sigi's part and
that Sigi had killed the thrall. He gathered men to look for Bredi,
and the search finally ended when they found him in the snowdrift.
Skadi said that thenceforth the snowdrift should be called Bredi's
drift, and ever since people have done this, calling every large drift
by that name.[3] It was thus revealed that Sigi had killed the thrall,
having committed murder.[4] He was then declared an outlaw, a
"wolf in hallowed places,"[5] and now he could no longer remain at
home with his father.

Then Odin guided Sigi out of the land on a journey so long
that it was remarkable. They continued until Odin brought him to
where some warships lay. Sigi next took to raiding with the troops
his father had given him before they parted, and he was victorious
in the raids. Matters progressed until in the end Sigi was able to

---

*Chapter titles with an asterisk have been supplied by the translator; all other
titles are in the original manuscript.

seize a kingdom to rule. Next he obtained a noble match for himself and became a great and powerful[6] king. He ruled over Hunland[7] and was a renowned warrior. By his wife, Sigi had a son who was called Rerir. The boy grew up there with his father and soon became big, strong, and able.

Now Sigi advanced in years, and many were envious of him. Finally, his wife's brothers, that is, they whom he most trusted, intrigued against him. They attacked and overwhelmed the king when he was least wary and had few men with him; in that encounter Sigi fell with all his men. His son Rerir was not present at the battle. Rerir gathered a large force of his friends and chieftains of the land, so that he was able to take over both the estates and the kingship that had belonged to his father Sigi.

When Rerir felt that he had established his footing in the kingdom he recalled his grievances against his maternal uncles, those who had killed his father. The king gathered a large force and marched against his kinsmen. He felt that they had already done him so much harm that he could place little value on their kinship. And so, with this reasoning he acted, not stopping until he had killed all his father's slayers, although such action was appalling by all accounts.[8] Then Rerir took over land, wealth, and power. He became an even more influential man than his father had been.

Now Rerir took much booty for himself, as well as the woman he thought most suitable for him. Although they lived together with intimacy for a long time, they had neither heir nor child. That lack displeased them both, and they fervently implored the gods that they might have a child. It is said that Frigg[9] heard their prayers and told Odin what they asked. Odin was not without resources. He called one of his wish maidens,[10] the daughter of the giant Hrimnir, and placed in her hand an apple, telling her to present it to the king. She took the apple, assumed the shape of a crow,[11] and flew until she reached the place where the king was sitting on a mound.[12] She let the apple fall into the king's lap. He took the apple, suspecting its purpose. Then he came back from the mound to his men. He visited with the queen and ate some of the apple.[13]

## 2    THE BIRTH OF VOLSUNG

Now there is this to tell: the queen soon discovered that she was carrying a child, and the pregnancy continued for a long time without her being able to give birth. Then there came a time when Rerir, as is the custom of kings, had to go on a campaign to pacify his land. On this journey it happened that Rerir took sick and soon died. He intended to go to Odin;[14] in those days that seemed desirable to many.

The queen's distress continued as before; she could not give birth to the child, and this affliction continued for six years. Then she recognized that she would not live long and asked that the child be cut from her. It was done as she requested. The child was a boy, and he was already well grown when born, as was to be expected. It is said that the boy kissed his mother before she died. He was given a name and called Volsung.[15] He was king over Hunland after his father. He was soon big, strong, and daring in what were thought to be tests of manhood and prowess. He became the greatest of warriors and was victorious in the battles he fought on his expeditions.

When Volsung was fully grown Hrimnir sent him his daughter Hljod, who was mentioned earlier, when she took the apple to Rerir, Volsung's father. Volsung married Hljod. They were together for a long time, well agreed and intimate. They had ten sons and one daughter. Their eldest son was called Sigmund, and the daughter was named Signy. They were twins, and in all things they were the foremost and the finest-looking of the children of King Volsung, though all of the other sons were imposing. It has long been remembered and highly spoken of that the descendants of Volsung were exceptionally ambitious. They surpassed most men named in old sagas in both knowledge and accomplishments and in the desire to win.

It is said that King Volsung had an excellent palace built in this fashion: a huge tree[16] stood with its trunk in the hall and its branches, with fair blossoms, stretched out through the roof. They called the tree Barnstock.[17]

## 3   SIGMUND DRAWS THE SWORD FROM BARNSTOCK*

There was a king called Siggeir who ruled over Gautland. He was a powerful king and had many followers. He paid a visit to King Volsung and asked for Signy's hand in marriage. The king took the proposal well, as did his sons, but Signy for her part was unwilling. Even so, she asked her father to make the decision, as he did in other matters that concerned her. It seemed advisable to the king to betroth her, and she was promised to King Siggeir. When the banquet and the marriage were to take place, King Siggeir was to feast at King Volsung's.

Using the best provisions, the king made ready for the feast. When the banquet was fully prepared the guests of King Volsung and King Siggeir came on the appointed day, and King Siggeir had many worthy men with him. It is said that large fires were kindled in the long hearths running the length of the hall, but in the middle of the hall stood the great tree that earlier was mentioned.

It is now told that when people were sitting by the fires in the evening a man came into the hall. He was not known to the men by sight. He was dressed in this way: he wore a mottled cape that was hooded; he was barefoot and had linen breeches tied around his legs. As he walked up to Barnstock he held a sword in his hand while over his head was a low-hanging hood. He was very tall and gray with age, and he had only one eye.[18] He brandished the sword and thrust it into the trunk so that it sank up to the hilt. Words of welcome failed everyone. Then the man began to speak: "He who draws this sword out of the trunk shall receive it from me as a gift, and he himself shall prove that he has never carried a better sword than this one."

Then this old man walked out of the hall, and nobody knew who he was or where he was going. They stood up now, and no one disputed whether or not to grasp the sword; each thought the one who reached it first would be best off. The noblest men went up to it first, and then each of the others. No one who came forward succeeded in moving it, no matter which way he tried. Now Sigmund, the son of King Volsung, came forward. He grasped the sword, and drew it from the trunk. It was as if the sword lay loose for him. The weapon seemed so good to everyone that no one recalled ever seeing so fine a sword. Siggeir offered to weigh Sigmund out triple the sword's weight in gold, to which Sigmund answered: "You could have taken this sword from where it stood, no less than I did, if it were meant for you to carry it; but now that it has come first into my hands, you will never obtain it, even should you offer me all the gold you own." King Siggeir became angry at these words and thought the answer scornful. But since he was a very underhanded and deceitful man, he pretended not to care about this matter. That same evening, however, he thought of a means of paying Sigmund back. And, this is what later came about.

## 4 Siggeir Plots Revenge*

Now there is this to be said: Siggeir went to bed with Signy that evening. The next day the weather was good. King Siggeir said that he wanted to return home rather than to wait until the wind rose or the sea became impassable. It is not told that King Volsung or his sons held King Siggeir back, especially when King Volsung saw that Siggeir wanted nothing other than to leave the feast.

Then Signy spoke to her father: "I do not wish to go away with Siggeir, nor do my thoughts laugh with him. I know through my foresight and that special ability found in our family[19] that if the marriage contract is not quickly dissolved, this union will bring us much misery." "You should not say such things, daughter," he replied, "for it would be shameful both for him and for us to break our agreement without cause. And if it is broken we could neither have his trust nor bind him in a friendly alliance. He would repay us with as much ill as he could. The one honorable thing is to hold to our side of the bargain."

King Siggeir prepared for the homeward voyage. Before he and his followers departed from the feast he invited King Volsung, his kinsman by marriage, to pay him a visit in Gautland in three months' time. King Volsung was invited with all his sons, and all the men that he wanted and thought befitting his dignity. By doing this King Siggeir wished to make up for his shortcomings in not staying more than one night during the wedding celebration, for it was not the custom of men to behave that way. King Volsung promised to make the journey and to come on the appointed day. The in-laws parted and King Siggeir traveled home with his wife.

## 5  THE FALL OF VOLSUNG

Now is the time to tell that King Volsung and his sons journeyed to Gautland at the appointed time, according to the invitation of their in-law, King Siggeir. They set off in three ships, all well manned, and the voyage went well. When they arrived off Gautland in their ships it was already late evening.

That same evening Signy, the daughter of King Volsung, came and called her father and brothers together for a private talk. She told them of King Siggeir's plans: that Siggeir had gathered an un-beatable army, "and he plans to betray you. Now I ask you," she said, "to return at once to your own kingdom and gather the largest force you can; then come back here and avenge yourselves. But, do not put yourselves in this trap, for you will not escape his treachery if you do not do as I advise."

King Volsung then spoke: "All peoples will bear witness that unborn I spoke one word and made the vow that I would flee neither fire nor iron from fear, and so I have done until now. Why should I not fulfill that vow in my old age? Maidens will not taunt my sons during games by saying that they feared their deaths, for each man must at one time die. No one may escape dying that once, and it is my counsel that we not flee, but for our own part act the bravest. I have fought a hundred times, sometimes with a larger army and sometimes with a lesser one. Both ways I have had the victory, and it will not be reported that I either fled or asked for peace."

Then Signy cried bitterly and asked that she might not be made to return to King Siggeir. King Volsung answered: "You must cer-tainly go home to your husband and be together with him, however it goes with us." Then Signy went home, and Volsung and his men remained there during the night. In the morning, as soon as dawn came, King Volsung ordered all his men to get up and go ashore, and to prepare for battle. They now all went on land fully armed, and they did not have long to wait before King Siggeir arrived with all his army. The hardest of battles took place between them; the king urged his men forward as fiercely as possible. It is said that King Volsung and his sons went through King Siggeir's ranks eight times that day, hewing on both sides. And when they intended to do so yet again, King Volsung fell in the middle of his ranks with all his men except for his ten sons. Because the force against them was overwhelming, they were forced to give way. His sons were seized and bound and taken away.

Signy learned that her father had been killed and her brothers taken prisoner and destined for death. She now asked King Siggeir to speak with her in private. Signy spoke: "I want to ask that you not have my brothers killed so quickly, but rather that you have them put in stocks. For it is with me as in the saying, 'the eye takes pleasure while it yet beholds.' I do not ask anything further for them, for I do not think it would be of any use." Then Siggeir answered her: "You are mad and out of your senses to plead for a worse misfortune for your brothers than that they be hewed down. But I will grant your request because I think it better that they suffer more and are tortured longer before they die."

Siggeir had Signy's wish carried out. A great trunk was brought and fitted as stocks on the feet of the ten brothers somewhere in the woods. They sat there all that day until night. But at midnight an old she-wolf came to them out of the woods as they sat in the stocks. She was both large and grim-looking. She bit one of the brothers to death and then ate him all up. After that she went away.

In the morning Signy sent her most trustworthy man to her brothers to learn what had occurred. And when he returned, he told her that one of them was dead. She thought it would be grievous if they all shared the same fate, but she could not help them. What happened can be quickly told; for nine nights in a row that same she-wolf came at midnight and each time killed and ate one of the brothers until all but Sigmund were dead. And now before the tenth night Signy sent her trusted man to her brother Sigmund. She gave him some honey and instructed him to smear it on Sigmund's face and to put some in his mouth. Her man went to Sigmund, did as he had been instructed, and then returned home.

As usual the same she-wolf came in the night, meaning to bite Sigmund to death as she had his brothers. But then she caught the scent of the honey that had been rubbed on him. She licked his face all over with her tongue and then reached her tongue into his mouth. He did not lose his composure and bit into the wolf's tongue. She jerked and pulled back hard, thrusting her feet against the trunk so that it split apart. But Sigmund held on so tightly that the wolf's tongue was torn out by the roots, and that was her death. And some men say that the she-wolf was Siggeir's mother, who had assumed this shape through witchcraft and sorcery.

## 6   SIGNY PLOTS REVENGE*

Now Sigmund is free, and the stocks are broken. He stayed there in the forest. Once again Signy sent men to find out what had taken place and if Sigmund was alive. And when they came, Sigmund told them all that had occurred between him and the she-wolf. Then they went home and told Signy of the events. She went and met with her brother and they decided that he should make an underground dwelling in the woods. Things went on for a while with Signy hiding him there and bringing him what he needed. King Siggeir, however, believed that all the Volsungs were dead.

King Siggeir had two sons by his wife. It is said that Signy sent the elder, when he was ten years old, to meet with Sigmund so that the boy could help if Sigmund wanted to try to avenge his father. The boy now went to the woods and late in the evening arrived at Sigmund's underground dwelling.[20] He was received well enough and told that he should make bread for them "and I will look for firewood." Sigmund handed him a sack of flour and went himself to look for wood. But when he returned the boy had done nothing about making the bread. Now Sigmund asked if the bread was ready and the boy answered: "I did not dare touch the flour sack because there is something alive in the meal." Sigmund now realized that this boy was not so stouthearted that he would want the lad with him.

When brother and sister next met, Sigmund said that he thought himself no closer to having a companion,[21] even though the boy was there with him. Signy answered: "Then take the boy and kill him. He need not live any longer." And so he did.

The winter passed, and the next winter Signy sent her younger son to meet with Sigmund. This story, however, does not need to be recounted at length, for things happened in much the same way, with Sigmund killing the boy at Signy's bidding.

# 7    SIGNY GIVES BIRTH TO SINFJOTLI

It is now told that once while Signy was sitting in her chamber, a sorceress, exceedingly skilled in the magic arts, came to her. Signy said to her: "I want the two of us to exchange shapes." The sorceress answered: "It shall be as you wish." And she used her craft so that they changed shapes. The sorceress now took Signy's place as Signy wished. She slept with the king that night, and he did not notice that it was not Signy beside him.

Now it is to be told of Signy that she went to her brother's underground dwelling and asked him to give her refuge for the night, "for I have lost my way out in the forest, and I do not know where I am going." He said that she could stay and that he would not refuse shelter to a woman alone, believing she would not repay his hospitality by betraying him. She entered his shelter and they sat down to eat. He frequently glanced at her and found her a fine and handsome woman. And when they had eaten their fill he told her that he wanted them to share one bed that night. She did not object and he had her next to him for three nights in a row. After that she returned home, met with the sorceress, and asked that they exchange shapes again, which the sorceress did.

And after a time Signy gave birth to a son. This son was called Sinfjotli. And when he grew up he was both large and strong, handsome of appearance, and very like the Volsung stock. He was not quite ten years old when Signy sent him to Sigmund in his underground shelter. Before sending her first sons to Sigmund, she had tested them by stitching the cuffs of their kirtles to their hands, passing the needle through both flesh and skin.[22] They withstood the ordeal poorly and cried out in pain. She also did this to Sinfjotli; he did not flinch. Then she ripped the kirtle from him, so that the skin followed the sleeves. She said that it must certainly be painful for him. He replied: "Such pain would seem trifling to Volsung."

Then the boy came to Sigmund. Sigmund asked him to knead their flour while he went to look for firewood. He handed the boy a sack and then went off for the wood. When he returned, Sinfjotli had finished the baking. Then Sigmund asked if he had discovered anything in the flour. "I am not without suspicion," he said, "that there was something alive in the flour when I first began kneading, but I have kneaded it in, whatever it was." Then Sigmund said and laughed as he spoke: "I do not think you should make your meal from this bread tonight, for you have kneaded into it the most poisonous of snakes." Sigmund was so hardy that he could eat poison with no ill effect. Sinfjotli, however, although he could tolerate poison externally, could neither eat nor drink it.

## 8    SIGMUND AND SINFJOTLI DON THE SKINS

It is now to be told that Sigmund thought Sinfjotli too young to seek vengeance with him, and that he first wanted to accustom the boy to hardship. During the summers they traveled widely through the forests, killing men for booty. It seemed to Sigmund that Sinfjotli took much after the Volsung race. Nevertheless, he believed the boy to be the son of King Siggeir and to have the evil disposition of his father along with the fierce zeal of the Volsungs. Sigmund felt that Sinfjotli did not put much store in kinship, for the boy often reminded Sigmund of his grievances, strongly urging the man to kill King Siggeir.

One time, they went again to the forest to get themselves some riches, and they found a house. Inside it were two sleeping men, with thick gold rings. A spell had been cast upon them: wolfskins hung over them in the house and only every tenth day could they shed the skins. They were the sons of kings. Sigmund and Sinfjotli put the skins on and could not get them off. And the weird power was there as before: they howled like wolves, both understanding the sounds. Now they set out into the forest, each going his own way. They agreed then that they would risk a fight with as many as seven men, but not with more, and that the one being attacked by more would howl with his wolf's voice. "Do not break this agreement," said Sigmund, "because you are young and daring, and men will want to hunt you."

Now each went his own way. And when they had parted, Sigmund found seven men and howled in his wolf's voice. Sinfjotli heard him, came at once, and killed them all. They parted again. Before Sinfjotli had traveled very far in the forest, he met with eleven men and fought them. In the end he killed them all. Badly wounded, Sinfjotli went under an oak tree to rest. Then Sigmund

came and said: "Why didn't you call?" Sinfjotli replied: "I did not
want to call you for help.[23] You accepted help to kill seven men. I
am a child in age next to you, but I did not ask for help in killing eleven men." Sigmund leapt at him so fiercely that Sinfjotli
staggered and fell. Sigmund bit him in the windpipe. That day they
were not able to come out of the wolfskins. Sigmund laid Sinfjotli
over his shoulder, carried him home to the hut, and sat over him.
He cursed the wolfskins, bidding the trolls to take them.

One day Sigmund saw two weasels. One bit the other in the
windpipe and then ran into the woods, returning with a leaf and
laying it on the wound. The other weasel sprang up healed. Sigmund went out and saw a raven[24] flying with a leaf. The raven
brought the leaf to Sigmund, who drew it over Sinfjotli's wound.
At once Sinfjotli sprang up healed, as if he had never been injured.

Then they went to the underground dwelling and stayed there
until they were to take off the wolfskins. They took the skins and
burned them in the fire, hoping that these objects would cause no
further harm. Under that magic spell they had performed many
feats in King Siggeir's kingdom. When Sinfjotli was fully grown Sigmund thought he had tested him fully.

It was not long before Sigmund wanted to seek vengeance for
his father Volsung, if it could be brought about. One day they left
the underground dwelling and came late in the evening to King
Siggeir's estate. They entered the outer room, which was in front
of the main hall. Inside the room were ale casks, and there they hid
themselves. The queen found out where they were and wanted to
meet with them. And when they met, they decided that when it
grew dark they would take revenge for their father.

Signy and the king had two young children. They played together in the hall with golden toys, rolling the toys along the floor
and running after them. One gold ring was flung farther out, into
the room where Sigmund and Sinfjotli were, and the boy ran after
the ring to look for it. Then he saw two large, fierce men sitting
there wearing long helmets and shining mail. He ran into the hall
to his father and told him what he had seen. The king suspected
treachery. Signy heard what they said. She rose up, took both children, went to the outer room to Sigmund and Sinfjotli and said they
should know that the children had betrayed them, "and I would
advise you to kill them."

Sigmund said: "I will not kill your children, even if they have betrayed me." But Sinfjotli did not falter. He drew his sword and killed both children, casting them into the hall in front of King Siggeir. The king now stood up and called on his followers to seize the men who had been hiding in the entrance hall all evening. Men ran out, wanting to seize them, but Sigmund and Sinfjotli defended themselves well and valiantly. For a long while the one who was nearest them thought himself to have it the worst. But at last Sigmund and Sinfjotli were overpowered and captured. They were bound and fettered, and there they sat all night.

Now the king considered what was the slowest death he could prepare for them. When morning came he had a large cairn built of stones and turf. When the mound was finished he had a huge stone slab set in the middle of the cairn so that one edge pointed upward and the other downward. The stone was so large that it reached both sides of the cairn and no one could go around it. Now he had Sigmund and Sinfjotli taken and put in the mound, one on each side of the stone, because he thought it worse for them not to be together, yet be able to hear each other. And when they were covering the mound with turf, Signy came up, holding some straw in her arms, and she threw it into the mound to Sinfjotli and told the thralls to conceal her act from the king. They agreed and then the mound was closed.

And when night came Sinfjotli spoke to Sigmund: "I do not thnk that our food will run short for a while, for the queen has thrown some pork wrapped in straw into the mound." And he felt the pork again and found that Sigmund's sword was stuck in it. He knew it by the hilt, for it was dark in the cairn. He told Sigmund and they both were overjoyed. Now Sinfjotli thrust the sword's point up over the rock and pulled hard. The sword bit into the slab. Sigmund grasped the point and they sawed the rock between them. They did not stop until the sawing was finished, as is told:

1.  They cut with might
    The massive slab,
    Sigmund, with his sword,
    And Sinfjotli.

They were now both loose together in the cairn and they sawed through both rock and iron, thus coming out of the mound. They went back to the hall. All the men were asleep. They carried wood to the hall and set the wood afire. Those inside woke up because of the smoke and the hall blazing around them. The king asked who had set the fire. "Here am I with Sinfjotli, my sister's son," said Sigmund, "and we now want for you to know that not all the Volsungs are dead."

Sigmund asked his sister to come out and receive from him esteem and great honor, for he wished in this way to amend her sorrows. She replied: "Now you shall know whether I remember the slaying of King Volsung by King Siggeir. I had our children killed when I thought them too slow in avenging our father, and I came to you in the forest in the shape of a sorceress, and Sinfjotli is our son. Because of this he has so much zeal; he is the child of both a son and a daughter of King Volsung. In everything I have worked toward the killing of King Siggeir. I have worked so hard to bring about vengeance that I am by no means fit to live. Willingly I shall now die with King Siggeir, although I married him reluctantly." Then she kissed her brother Sigmund and Sinfjotli, walked into the fire, and wished them farewell. She died there with King Siggeir and all the retainers.

The kinsmen, Sigmund and Sinfjotli, gathered together men and ships, and Sigmund set out for his patrimony. There he expelled from the country the king who had set himself up as ruler after King Volsung. Sigmund now became a rich and excellent king, wise and ambitious. He married a woman called Borghild. They had two sons, one named Helgi and the other Hamund. And when Helgi was born, Norns[25] came and set his destiny, saying that he would become the most famous of all kings. Sigmund had returned from battle and went with a leek[26] to meet his son. He gave the boy the name Helgi, and as gifts for this name-fastening he granted Hringstead, Solfell,[27] and a sword. He bid the child to advance himself well and to take after the race of the Volsungs. Helgi grew to be magnanimous and well loved and surpassed most other men in all accomplishments. It is said that he went warring when he was fifteen years old. Helgi was king over the troops, and Sinfjotli was asked to accompany him. Both commanded the men.

## 9   HELGI MARRIES SIGRUN

It is said that, while raiding, Helgi came across the king called Hunding. He was a powerful king with a large following and ruled over a country.[28] It came to a battle between them. Helgi pushed resolutely forward, and the battle ended with Helgi as the victor; King Hunding fell with a great many of his men. Helgi now saw his status increase considerably by having killed so powerful a king.

In order to avenge their father, Hunding's sons now raised an army against Helgi. They engaged in a fierce battle, and Helgi fought his way through the brothers' ranks, attacking their standards. Of Hunding's sons, he killed Alf and Eyjolf, Hervard and Hagbard, and here he won a renowned victory.

And when Helgi left the battle, he found many women of worthy appearance by the edge of a forest. They were riding in magnificent attire. Yet one of them, she who was in the lead, surpassed all the others, and Helgi asked for her name. She called herself Sigrun and said she was the daughter of King Hogni. Helgi said: "Accompany us home and be welcome."

Then the king's daughter replied: "We have a different task before us from drinking with you." Helgi asked: "What might that be, princess?" She answered: "King Hogni has promised me to Hodbrodd, the son of King Granmar. But I have sworn that I would no sooner have him than a young crow. Yet the marriage will take place unless you stop Hodbrodd. Fight him with your army and take me away, because there is no king with whom I would rather dwell than with you." "Be of good cheer, princess," Helgi said. "We would sooner try our valor than have you marry him. We shall first see which of us overcomes the other—I stake my life on this."

Then Helgi sent men with gifts of value to call up followers, and he summoned all his troops to Raudabjorg. Helgi waited there until a mighty company came to him from Hedinsey. Then a large troop came to him from Norvasund[29] in big and handsome ships. King Helgi called his ship's captain, named Leif, to him and asked if he had counted their army. But the man replied: "It is not easy to count, my lord. The ships that have come from Norvasund have twelve thousand men, but the other troop is half again larger."

Then King Helgi said that they should turn into the fjord called Varinsfjord, and this they did. A violent storm broke upon them with seas so high that the waves crashing against the hulls sounded like cliffs colliding. Helgi told the men not to fear and not to reef the sails, but rather to set each sail higher than before. They were on the point of foundering before they could reach land. Then Sigrun, the daughter of King Hogni, came down to the coast with a large following and directed Helgi and his men to a good harbor called Gnipalund. The men of the country saw these events and King Hodbrodd's brother, the one who ruled Svarinshaug, also came down to the coast. He called to them and asked who was leading that large force. Sinfjotli stood up, his helmet shining like glass on his head, his coat of mail white as snow, his spear in his hand adorned with a magnificent banner, and his shield rimmed with gold before him. This man knew how to speak with kings.[30] "When you have fed your pigs and hounds and you meet your wife, say that the Volsungs have come and King Helgi can be found here in the army, if Hodbrodd wants to meet him. And it is Helgi's pleasure to fight with distinction while you kiss your bondwomen by the fire."

Granmar[31] answered: "You are not able to say much of worth or speak of ancient lore,[32] since you lie about noble men. More likely it is that you long nourished yourself on the food of wolves out in the forest and killed your brothers. And it is strange that you dare to come in an army with good men, you who have sucked the blood of many cold corpses."

Sinfjotli replied: "You probably do not remember clearly now when you were the witch on Varinsey and said that you wanted to marry a man and you chose me for the role of husband. And afterward you were a valkyrie in Asgard[33] and all were on the verge of fighting for your sake. I sired nine wolves on you at Laganess, and I was the father of them all."

Granmar responded: "You are a great liar. I do not think you could sire anyone because you were gelded by the giant's daughters on Thrasness. You are the stepson of King Siggeir and you lay in the woods with wolves, and all misfortunes came to you one on top of the other. You killed your brothers and made for yourself an evil reputation."

Sinfjotli answered: "Do you remember when you were a mare with the stallion Grani[34] and I rode you at full speed on Bravoll? Afterward you were the goatherd of the giant Golnir." Granmar said: "I would rather feed the birds on your corpse than quarrel with you any longer." Then King Helgi said: "It would be better and more clever for you both to fight, rather than to speak in a manner that is shameful to hear. Granmar's sons are no friends of mine, but still they are hardy men."

Granmar now rode away to meet with King Hodbrodd at the place called Solfell. Their horses were named Sveipud and Sveggjud. They met at the fortress gate and King Hodbrodd was told the war news. Hodbrodd was in his mail coat with his helmet on his head. He asked who they were—"and why are you so angry?" Granmar said: "The Volsungs have come here with twelve thousand men near shore and seven thousand by the island called Sok, but they have the largest force at the place called Grindir.[35] And I think that Helgi will now want to fight." The king responded: "Let us send a call through all our kingdom and proceed against them. No one shall sit at home who wants to fight. Let us send word to the sons of Hring and to King Hogni and to Alf the Old. They are all great warriors."

They met at the place called Frekastein and a savage battle ensued. Helgi pushed forward through his opponents' ranks. A great many men fell there. Then they saw a large band of shield-maidens[36]—it was like looking into a fire; Sigrun the king's daughter had arrived. King Helgi advanced against King Hodbrodd and killed him beneath his own standard. Then Sigrun said: "Receive my thanks for this brave deed. Lands will now find new owners. This is a most fortunate day for me, and you will receive glory and fame for killing so powerful a king."

King Helgi assumed power in that kingdom and lived there a long time. He married Sigrun and became a famous and excellent king. And he is out of the saga.

## 10    CONCERNING THE VOLSUNGS

The Volsungs now journeyed home, having once again greatly increased their reputation. Sinfjotli set off raiding again. He saw a lovely woman and strongly desired to have her. The brother of Borghild, the wife of King Sigmund, had also asked for her hand. They contested the issue in a battle and Sinfjotli slew this king. He now went raiding far and wide, fought many battles, and was always the victor. He became the most renowned and celebrated of men and returned home in the fall with many ships and much wealth. He told his father what had happened, and the king told the queen. She asked Sinfjotli to leave the kingdom, saying she did not want to see him. Sigmund said he would not let him go away and offered to compensate her loss with gold and great wealth, even though he had never before paid compensation for a man. He said there was no distinction to be had in contending with women. When she could not have her way she said: "You shall decide, sir, as is fitting."

With the king's consent Borghild now arranged her brother's funeral feast, preparing for the banquet with the best of provisions. She invited many important men, and she herself served the drink. She came before Sinfjotli with a large drinking horn, saying: "Drink now, stepson." He accepted the horn, looked inside, and said: "The drink is fouled." Sigmund said: "Give it to me, then." He drank it down.

The queen said: "Why should other men drink ale for you?" She came again with the drinking horn. "Drink now." And she taunted him with many words. He took the horn and said: "The drink is mixed with treachery." Sigmund said: "Then give it to me." She came a third time and bid him drain it, if he had the heart of a Volsung. Sinfjotli took the horn and said: "There is poison in this drink." Sigmund answered: "Filter it through your mustache, son." The king was quite drunk, and therefore he talked in this way.

Sinfjotli drank and at once fell to the ground. Sigmund rose and his sorrow was almost his death. He took the body in his arms and went into the woods, coming at last to a fjord. There he saw a man in a small boat. The man asked if he wanted to accept from him passage across the fjord. Sigmund said yes. The boat was so small that it would not bear them all, so the body was carried first and Sigmund walked along the fjord. The next moment the boat and the man disappeared before Sigmund's eyes.[37] After that Sigmund returned home, and now he drove the queen out. A short time later she died. King Sigmund continued to rule over his kingdom and is thought to have been the greatest champion and king in ancient times.

## *11*    SIGMUND MARRIES HJORDIS*

There was a king named Eylimi. He was powerful and famous. His daughter was named Hjordis, the fairest and wisest of all women. King Sigmund heard that she and none other was the match for him.

Sigmund set out to visit King Eylimi. King Eylimi prepared a great feast for Sigmund, to be held on the condition that Sigmund had not come with the intention of fighting. Messages were exchanged between them confirming that the purpose this time was friendship and not war. The banquet was prepared with the best provisions and many people were present. Everywhere he went King Sigmund was provided with a marketplace[38] and given other amenities for his journey. They arrived now at the feast and the two kings shared the one hall. King Lyngvi, the son of King Hunding, had also come. He, too, wanted to become King Eylimi's son-in-law. It was apparent to King Eylimi that both men could not succeed in the same errand, and he also thought it likely that trouble might be expected from the one who failed.

Then the king said to his daughter: "You are a wise woman, and I have said that you shall choose your own husband. Choose now between these two kings and I will decide as you do." She answered: "The decision is difficult. Yet I choose the most famous king, and that is King Sigmund, although he is very old." Thus she was given to Sigmund, and King Lyngvi went away. Sigmund was married, receiving Hjordis as his bride. Each successive day they feasted better and with more zeal. After this King Sigmund returned home to Hunland and his father-in-law King Eylimi came with him, and Sigmund now tended to his kingdom.[39]

King Lyngvi and his brothers now gathered an army and went against King Sigmund, because, although they had always received the short end in their previous dealings, this new development was one too many. Now they intended to destroy the pride of the Volsungs. They arrived in Hunland and sent word to King Sigmund. They did not want to sneak up on him, and they were certain that he would not run away. King Sigmund said he would come to battle, and he gathered an army. But Hjordis, together with a bondwoman and great wealth, was driven to a forest. There Hjordis stayed during the fighting.

The Vikings leapt from their ships with an unconquerable army. King Sigmund and Eylimi raised their banners and then the trumpets were blown. King Sigmund now let sound his horn, the one his father had owned, and urged his men onward. Sigmund had a much smaller force. A fierce battle commenced, and, although Sigmund was old, he fought hard and was always at the front of his men. Neither shield nor mail coat could withstand him, and again and again that day he went through the ranks of his enemies, and no one could foresee how it would end between them. Many a spear and arrow was cast in the air. Sigmund's spaewomen,[40] however, shielded him so well that he remained unscathed, and no one could count how many men fell before him. Both his arms were bloody to the shoulder.

The battle had been going on for some time, when a man came into the fight. He had a wide-brimmed hat that sloped over his face, and he wore a black hooded cloak. He had one eye, and he held a spear in his hand.[41] This man came up against King Sigmund, raising the spear before him. When Sigmund struck hard with his sword, it broke in two against the spear. Then the tide of the battle turned, for King Sigmund's luck was now gone, and many of his men fell. The king did not seek to protect himself and fiercely urged his men on. Now it was as they say: no one is able against many.

## 12    HJORDIS REMARRIES*

King Sigmund, along with King Eylimi, his father-in-law, fell in this battle at the head of his troops. The larger part of Sigmund's force fell with him. King Lyngvi now advanced toward the royal estate with the intention of seizing the princess, but in this he failed. He obtained there neither woman nor wealth. He traveled now through the land and placed his men throughout the kingdom. He believed that he had killed all of the Volsung kin and that nothing more was to be feared from them.

That night, after the battle, Hjordis went out among the slain and came to where King Sigmund lay. She asked if he could be healed. He, however, answered: "Many a man lives where there is little hope, but my luck has forsaken me, so that I do not want to let myself be healed. Odin does not want me to wield the sword

since it is now broken. I have fought battles while it pleased him."
She answered: "I would lack nothing, if you were healed and took
revenge for my father."

The king said: "That is intended for another. You are carrying
a son. Raise him well and carefully, for he will be an excellent boy,
the foremost of our line. Guard well the broken pieces of the sword.
From them can be made a good sword, which will be called Gram.
Our son will bear it and with it accomplish many great deeds,
which will never be forgotten. And his name will endure while the
world remains. I am content with this. But my wounds tire me and
I will now visit our kinsmen who have gone on before."

Hjordis sat by him now until he died, and then day was breaking. She saw that many ships had landed. She spoke to her slave
woman: "We will exchange clothes, and you shall use my name and
say you are a king's daughter." And this they did.

The Vikings could see the great carnage and also the women
heading for the woods. They recognized that an important event
had occurred and so they leapt from the ships. Alf, the son of King
Hjalprek of Denmark, led this force. He had sailed along the coast
with his army. They reached the battlefield and saw there the large
number of dead. King Alf now issued orders to look for the women
and this was done. He asked the women who they were, as little
could be distinguished from their appearance. The bondwoman
answered for them both. She told of the fall of King Sigmund and
King Eylimi along with many other great men and said who had
caused this. Alf asked if they knew where the king's treasure was
concealed.

The bondwoman replied: "It is certainly to be expected that
we would know." And she showed them the way to the treasure.
They found enormous wealth, so much that the men thought they
had never seen an equal amount gathered in one place, or more precious things. They carried the wealth to King Alf's ships. Hjordis
and the slave woman followed him. He now returned to his kingdom and made known that those kings had fallen who were the
most famous of men. The king sat at the helm of the ship and the
women sat on the first bench. He spoke with them and listened
carefully to what they said.

The king returned home to his kingdom with much wealth. Alf
was the most able of men. And when he had been home a short

while, the queen asked her son Alf: "Why does the fairer woman wear fewer rings and lesser clothing? It seems to me that she is nobler whom you have made less of." He replied: "I have suspected that her manner is not that of a servingwoman's. When we first met, she well knew how to greet men of rank. I shall put this to a test."

Now one time while they were drinking, the king talked with the women and said: "How do you note the break of day, when the night grows light, if you can not see the heavenly bodies?" The maidservant answered: "This is how I note it: as a child I was in the habit of drinking quite a bit before dawn. And when I stopped doing that, I would still wake up at the same time, and that is my signal." The king smiled at this reply and said: "That is a poor habit for a king's daughter."

Then he turned to Hjordis and asked her the same. She answered him: "My father gave me a small gold ring with this characteristic: Just before daybreak[42] it becomes cold on my finger. That is how I know." The king answered: "Gold was certainly abundant if the serving girls wore it. And you have hidden from me long enough. I would have treated you as if we were both children of the same king, if you had told me. But I shall treat you in even a better way, as you deserve. You shall be my wife and I shall pay your dowry, when you have given birth to a child." She replied and told the complete truth about her situation. She stayed there now with much honor and was thought the most worthy of women.

## _13_ THE BIRTH OF SIGURD

It is now said that Hjordis gave birth to a son and the boy was brought before Alf's father, King Hjalprek. The king was pleased when he saw the boy's piercing eyes, and he said that none would be his like or equal. The child was sprinkled with water and named Sigurd. All say one thing about him: that none was his match in conduct and size. He was raised there with King Hjalprek, and all showed him great affection. And when all the most renowned men and kings in the ancient sagas are named, Sigurd must be counted the foremost in strength and accomplishments, in zeal and valor.

Of these qualities he possessed more than any other man in the northern world. Sigurd grew up there with Hjalprek and was loved by everyone. Hjalprek betrothed Hjordis to King Alf and fixed her dowry.

Regin, the son of Hreidmar, was Sigurd's foster father.[43] He taught Sigurd sports, chess, and runes.[44] Among many other things, he also taught Sigurd to speak in several tongues, as was the custom for a king's son. One time, when they were both together, Regin asked Sigurd if he knew how much wealth his father had had and who was guarding it. Sigurd answered and said that the kings watched over it. Regin said: "Do you trust them completely?" Sigurd replied: "It is fitting that they guard it as long as it suits me, for they can watch over it better than I."

Regin came another time to talk to Sigurd and said: "It is strange that you want to be the stableboy of kings or to go about like a vagrant." Sigurd answered: "That is not true, for I rule over everything with them. I can take whatever I want." Regin said: "Ask him to give you a horse." "It will be done as soon as I wish," answered Sigurd.

Sigurd met now with the kings. Then the king said to Sigurd, "What do you want from us?" Sigurd replied: "I would accept a horse for my entertainment." The king said: "Choose yourself a horse and anything else you want that we possess."

The next day Sigurd went to the forest and met an old man with a long beard. The man was unknown to Sigurd. He asked where Sigurd was going. Sigurd answered: "I am going to choose a horse. Advise me in this." The man responded: "Let us go and drive them to the river called Busiltjorn."

They drove the horses out into the deep river and all swam ashore but one; Sigurd took this one. It was gray in color, young in age, very large and handsome. No one had ever mounted this steed. The bearded man said: "This horse is descended from Sleipnir.[45] He must be raised carefully, because he will become better than any other horse." The man disappeared then. Sigurd called the horse Grani, and he was the best horse there ever was. It was Odin whom Sigurd had met.

Again Regin spoke to Sigurd: "You have too little wealth. It vexes me that you run around like a messenger boy. But I can tell you where there is great wealth to be had. And it is likely that there

would be honor in seeking it and glory should you acquire it."
Sigurd asked where this wealth might be and who was watching
over it.

Regin answered: "He is named Fafnir, and he is lying a short
way from here at a place called Gnitaheath. When you get there,
you will say that never have you seen in one place more riches in
gold. And you will not need more, even if you become the oldest
and most famous of kings."

Sigurd answered: "Although I am young, I know the nature
of this serpent,[46] and I have heard that no one dare go against him
because of his size and ferocity." Regin replied: "That is not true.
His size is no different from that of other grass snakes and more
is made of it than it deserves. And so it would have seemed to your
forefathers. Although you are of the Volsung stock, you do not appear to have the spirit of that kin, which is figured the foremost in
every form of distinction."

Sigurd said: "It may be that I do not have much of their valor
or skill, but there is no need to taunt me when I am yet little past
childhood. But why do you urge me on so strongly?" Regin replied:
"There is a tale behind this, and I will tell it to you." "Let me hear
it," said Sigurd.

## _14_ THE OTTER'S RANSOM*

"This tale begins with my father, who was named Hreidmar, a
great and wealthy man. One of his sons was named Fafnir, another
Otr, and I was the third, the least accomplished and the least hon-
ored. I knew how to work iron as well as silver and gold, and from
everything I could make something useful. My brother Otr had a
different occupation and nature. He was a great fisherman and surpassed other men in this skill. He had the likeness of an otter during
the day and was always in the river bringing up fish in his mouth.
He brought his catch to his father and thus greatly helped him. He
was in many ways like an otter. He came home late and ate alone
with his eyes shut, because he could not stand seeing his food di-
minish. Fafnir was by far the largest and the fiercest of the sons,
and he wanted to call everything his own.

"There was a dwarf named Andvari," said Regin. "He was always in the waterfall called Andvari's Fall. He was in the shape of a pike and caught food there for himself, for there were many fish in the falls. My brother Otr used to go into the waterfall and bring up fish in his mouth, laying them one by one on the bank. Odin, Loki,[47] and Hœnir[48] were traveling and came to Andvari's Fall. Otr had caught a salmon and was eating it, half dozing on the riverbank. Loki took a stone and struck the otter to death. The Æsir[49] considered themselves fortunate in their catch and skinned the otter.

"That evening they came to Hreidmar's and showed him the catch. Then we seized them, imposing as their fine and ransom that they must fill the skin with gold and cover the outside with red gold. They sent Loki to obtain the gold. He went to Ran[50] and got her net. Next he went to Andvari's Fall and cast the net out for the pike, and it leapt into the net. Then Loki said,

2.   Which is the fish
     That runs through the flood,
     And knows not to guard himself from danger?
     Your head,
     Ransom it from Hel[51]
     And find me the fire of the well.[52]

3.   Andvari is my name,
     Odin[53] was my father;
     Many a falls have I fared over.
     A wretched Norn
     Destined in ancient days
     That I should wade in water.

"Loki saw Andvari's gold. And when Andvari had handed over the gold he kept one ring back. But Loki took it from him. The dwarf went into the rock and said that the gold ring would be the death of whoever owned it, and the same applied to all the gold.

"The Æsir delivered the riches to Hreidmar, stuffed the otter skin, and set it on its feet. They then had to pile up the gold next to it and cover the outside. And when that was done, Hreidmar came forward and saw one whisker and demanded that it be covered. Then Odin drew the ring, Andvaranaut,[54] from his hand and covered the hair. Then Loki said,

4.  With gold you are now paid
    And as payment you have
    Much for my head.
    No ease
    Is assigned to your son;
    Death it is to you both.

"Afterward Fafnir killed his father," continued Regin, "and it was murder since he hid the body. I obtained none of the treasure. Fafnir became so ill-natured that he set out for the wilds and allowed no one to enjoy the treasure but himself. He has since become the most evil serpent and lies now upon this hoard. Afterward I traveled to the king and became his smith. And this is the story of how I lost the legacy of my father and compensation for my brother. Gold has since then been called Otter's Ransom and is spoken of as such."

Sigurd answered: "You have lost much, and your kinsmen have been vile."

## 15   REGIN FASHIONS GRAM

Sigurd said: "Make a sword now with your skill so that its equal has never been made. Do this and I will be able to work great deeds if courage helps, and if you want me to kill this dragon." Regin said: "With confidence I shall make it and you will be able to kill Fafnir with this sword."

Regin now made a sword.[55] He gave it to Sigurd, who took it and said: "This is your smithying, Regin." Sigurd struck the anvil and the sword broke. He threw down the blade and told Regin to forge another, better one.

Regin made a second sword and brought it to Sigurd. He considered it. "You will like this one, though you are a hard man to forge for." Sigurd tried the sword and he broke it like the first one. Then Sigurd said to Regin: "You are untrustworthy, just like your forefathers."

Sigurd went now to his mother. She greeted him well. They talked with each other and drank. Then Sigurd said: "Have I heard rightly that King Sigmund gave you the sword Gram in two pieces?" "That is true," she replied. "Give it to me," Sigurd said. "I wish to have it."

She said he was likely to win renown and gave him the sword. Sigurd met now with Regin and told him to make a sword worthy of these fragments. Regin became angry and went to his forge with the pieces of the sword. He thought Sigurd demanding about the metalwork. Now Regin made a sword. And when he brought it out of the forge, it seemed to the apprentices as if flames were leaping from its edges. He told Sigurd to take the sword and said he was no swordsmith if this one broke. Sigurd hewed at the anvil and split it to its base. The blade did not shatter or break. He praised the sword highly and went to the river with a tuft of wool, which he threw in against the current. The sword cut the wool in two when the tuft ran against the blade. Sigurd went home contented.

Regin said: "You must fulfill your vow, now that I have made the sword, and go to meet Fafnir." Sigurd replied: "I will fulfill it, but first there is another task; I must avenge my father." The older Sigurd grew, the more he was loved, and every mother's child held him dear.

## 16    GRIPIR FORETELLS SIGURD'S FUTURE*

There was a man named Gripir, the brother of Sigurd's mother. Soon after the sword had been made, Sigurd went to meet with Gripir because this uncle could see into the future and knew the fate of men. Sigurd asked Gripir how his life would go. For a long time Gripir was unwilling to answer, but finally, yielding to Sigurd's fervent pleas, he told him his whole fate, exactly as it later came to pass. And when Gripir had told him these things, as he had asked, Sigurd rode home. Soon afterward he and Regin met, and Regin said: "Kill Fafnir, as you have promised." Sigurd answered: "I shall do that, but first I must do something else: avenge King Sigmund and my other relatives who fell in that battle."

## *17* SIGURD KILLS LYNGVI AND HJORVARD AND ALL THE OTHERS

Now Sigurd met with the kings and said to them: "I have been here awhile, and I am indebted to you for your affection and esteem. But now I want to leave this country and find the sons of Hunding. I want them to know that the Volsungs are not all dead. I would like your support in this undertaking."

The kings said they would supply everything that Sigurd asked for. A large force was prepared. Everything was arranged most carefully, both ships and all the armaments, so that his expedition would be more magnificent than any before. Sigurd captained the largest and most splendid dragon ship. The sails were elaborately worked and glorious to see. The men sailed with a fair wind.

And when a few days had passed, the weather grew foul and a great storm arose, churning the sea as if it were foaming with blood. Although the sails might rip, Sigurd did not order them shortened; rather he commanded each sail to be set higher than before. And when they sailed by a certain craggy headland a man called up to the ship and asked who was in command of the army. He was told that their leader was Sigurd, the son of Sigmund, now the most famous of young men.

The man answered: "Everyone says one thing about him, that no king's son can equal him. I would like you to lower the sails on one of your ships and take me with you." They asked his name, and he answered:

5. As Hnikar they hailed me
  When Hugin I gladdened[56]
  And when, O young Volsung,
  I vanquished.
  Now you may address
  The old man of this rock
  As Feng or Fjolnir.[57]
  From here I would take passage.

They turned toward land and took the old man aboard. The wind now subsided and they sailed until they landed in the kingdom of the sons of Hunding. Then Fjolnir disappeared. At once they unleashed fire and iron, killing men and burning settlements, destroying as they went. Many fled from them to King Lyngvi and told him that an army had come to the land and was advancing with more ferocity than had ever before been seen. They said that the sons of Hunding had not been farsighted when they claimed that the Volsungs need not be feared: "for now Sigurd the son of Sigmund is leading the army."

King Lyngvi summoned men to arms throughout his kingdom. He refused to flee, and he called to his side every man who would support him. He and his brothers went against Sigurd with a mighty force, and then the fiercest of battles began between them. Masses of spears and arrows could be seen flying through the air; axes swung violently, shields were split, armor was cut open, helmets were slashed, and skulls were cloven. Many men fell to the ground.

When the battle had gone on a very long time, Sigurd advanced past the standards, holding in his hand the sword Gram. He hewed both men and horses and went through the ranks, so that both his arms were bloody to the shoulder. People fled from him as he advanced, and neither helmet nor mail coat withstood him. No one thought he had ever seen such a man before. The battle lasted a long time, with heavy slaughter and fierce encounters. And it happened there, as is unusual when the home army attacks, that it could not advance. So many fell from the ranks of the sons of Hunding that no one knew their number. And Sigurd was at the front of his troops. Then the sons of King Hunding attacked him. Sigurd struck at King Lyngvi and split his helmet and his head and his armored body. After that he cut Lyngvi's brother Hjorvard into two pieces. Then he killed all the sons of Hunding who were still alive, along with the larger part of their army.

Sigurd now returned home with a fine victory and the great wealth and glory he had obtained in this venture. Banquets were prepared for him in the kingdom. When Sigurd had been home a short time, Regin came to speak with him and said: "Now you will want to strike the helmet from Fafnir, as you have promised, because you have now avenged your father and your other kinsmen." Sigurd answered: "I will fulfill my promise; it will not escape my thoughts."

## *18*     REGIN AND SIGURD GO RIDING

Now Sigurd and Regin rode up onto the heath and onto the track along which Fafnir was accustomed to crawl when he went to drink. And it is said that this cliff was thirty fathoms high at the spot where Fafnir lay to get water. Then Sigurd said: "You told me, Regin, that this dragon was no larger than a serpent, but his tracks seem excessively large to me." Regin said: "Dig a ditch and sit in it, and then, when the serpent crawls to the water, pierce him in the heart and thus cause his death. You will win great renown from such a deed." Sigurd asked: "But what will happen, if I get in the way of the dragon's blood?" "No one can advise you, if you are afraid of everything. You are not like your kin in courage," replied Regin.

Now Sigurd rode onto the heath, and Regin ran off in fear. Sigurd dug a ditch. And while he was working on it, an old man with a long beard[58] came to him and asked what he was doing. Sigurd told him. Then the old man responded: "That is ill-advised. Dig several ditches for the blood to run into; then you sit in one of them and thrust at the heart of the worm." Then this man disappeared. And Sigurd dug the ditches in the manner described to him.

When the worm crawled to the water the earth quaked mightily, so that all the ground nearby shook. He blew poison over all the path before him, but Sigurd was neither afraid of nor concerned by the din. And when the serpent crawled over the pit, Sigurd plunged the sword up under the left shoulder, so that it sank to the hilt. Then Sigurd leapt up out of the ditch, and drew the sword out of the serpent. His arms were all bloody to the shoulder. And when the huge worm felt his mortal wound he thrashed his head and his tail, destroying everything that got in his way.

And when Fafnir received his death wound, he asked: "Who are you, or who is your father, or who is your family, you who are so impudent that you dare to bear weapons against me?" Sigurd replied: "My family is unknown to men. I am called the noble beast.[59] I have neither father nor mother, and I have traveled alone." Fafnir answered: "If you have neither father nor mother, from what wonder were you born? And although you will not tell me your name on my dying day, you know that you are lying." He answered: "My name is Sigurd and my father is Sigmund."

Fafnir then asked: "Who urged you on to this deed, and why did you let yourself be persuaded? Have you not heard that all people are afraid of me and my helm of terror?[60] Boy with the sharp eyes, you had a keen father." Sigurd said: "A hard mind whetted me for this deed and I was supported in it by this strong hand and this sharp sword, which you are now familiar with. Few are bold in old age who are cowardly in childhood."

Fafnir said: "I know that if you had grown up with your kinsmen you would know how to fight when angered. But it is yet stranger that a prisoner taken in war should have dared to fight me, because few captives are valiant in a fight." Sigurd spoke: "You revile me for being removed from my kinsmen. Even though I was taken in war, I was not bound, and you have discovered that I was free." Fafnir answered: "You take everything I say as spoken with malice. But this gold that was mine will be your death." Sigurd replied: "Everyone wants to have wealth until that one day, but everyone must die sometime." Fafnir said: "You do not want to heed my advice, but you will drown if you voyage unwarily by sea. Remain instead on land until it is calm."

Sigurd said: "Tell me, Fafnir, if you are so wise, who are the Norns, who separate sons from their mothers?" Fafnir replied: "They are many and sundry. Some are of the race of Æsir, some are of the race of elves, and some are the daughters of Dvalin."[61] Sigurd said: "What is the name of that island where Surt and the Æsir will mix together their blood?"[62] Fafnir answered: "It is called Oskapt, the uncreated."

And again Fafnir spoke: "My brother Regin caused my death, but it gladdens me that he will also cause your death. And it will go as he wishes." Again Fafnir spoke: "I have borne a helm of terror over all people since I lay on my brother's inheritance. And I blew poison in all directions around me, so that none dared come near me, and I feared no weapon. I never found so many men before me that I did not think myself much stronger, and everyone was afraid of me." Sigurd said: "This helm of terror you speak of gives victory to few, because each man who finds himself in company with many others must at one time discover that no one is the boldest of all."

Fafnir answered: "I suggest you take your horse and ride away as fast as you can, because it often happens that he who receives a mortal wound avenges himself." Sigurd said: "That is your advice, but I will do otherwise. I will ride to your den and there take the massive hoard of gold which your kin possessed." Fafnir replied: "You will ride there, where you will find so much gold that it will be plentiful for the rest of your days. And that same gold will be your death, as it will be the death of all who possess it." Sigurd stood up and said: "I would ride home, even though it would mean losing this great treasure, if I knew that I would never die. But every brave man wants to be wealthy until that one day. And you, Fafnir, lie in your death throes until Hel has you." Then Fafnir died.

## 19    REGIN DRINKS FAFNIR'S BLOOD

After Fafnir died Regin came to Sigurd and said: "Hail, my lord. You have won a great victory, as you have killed Fafnir. None before were so bold as to dare to sit in his path. And this glorious feat will live on while the world remains." Regin stood and looked down at the ground for a long time. Then afterward he said with much emotion: "You have killed my brother, but I am hardly blameless in this deed."

Sigurd took his sword Gram, dried it off on the grass, and said to Regin: "You went quite far away when I performed this deed. I tested this sharp sword with my own hand, pitting my strength against the serpent's might, while you lay in a heather bush confused, not knowing whether it was heaven or earth." Regin answered: "That serpent might have lain a long time in his den, if you had not enjoyed the sword I made for you with my own hands. Neither you nor anyone else would yet have accomplished this deed." Sigurd replied: "When men come to battle, a fearless heart serves a man better than a sharp sword." Then out of deep sorrow Regin repeated to Sigurd: "You have killed my brother and I can hardly be considered blameless in this deed."

Then Sigurd cut the heart out of the serpent with the sword called Ridill. Regin drank Fafnir's blood and said: "Grant me one request, a trifle for you. Go to the fire with the heart, roast it, and give it to me to eat." Sigurd went and roasted Fafnir's heart on a spit. And when the juice foamed out he tested it with his finger to see whether it was done. He stuck his finger in his mouth. And when the blood from the serpent's heart touched his tongue, he could understand the speech of birds. He heard the nuthatches chirping in the brush near him.

## 20   SIGURD EATS THE SERPENT'S HEART

"There sits, Sigurd, roasting Fafnir's heart. Better he should eat it himself," said a bird. "Then he would be wiser than any man." Another said: "There lies Regin, who wants to betray the one who trusts him." Then a third spoke: "He should strike Regin's head off; then he alone would control the huge store of gold." Then a fourth spoke: "Sigurd would be wise to follow their advice. Afterward he should ride to Fafnir's den and take the magnificent hoard of gold which is there, and then ride up to Hindarfell, where Brynhild sleeps. There he will find great wisdom. He would be wise to take your advice and consider his own needs. I suspect a wolf where I see a wolf's ears." Then a fifth said: "He is not as wise as I thought if he spares Regin after having killed his brother." Then a sixth spoke: "It would be a wise course if Sigurd killed Regin and took the treasure for himself."

Then Sigurd said: "It will not be my ill fate that Regin shall be my death. Rather, both brothers should go the same way." He now drew the sword Gram and cut off Regin's head. After that he ate some of the serpent's heart and kept some. He then leapt onto his horse and rode along Fafnir's trail until he came to the lair, which he found open. All the doors were made of iron, as were all their fastenings. All the posts in the house were also of iron, and they had been sunk into the earth. There Sigurd found an enormous store of gold, as well as the sword Hrotti. He took from there the helm of terror, the golden coat of chain mail, and many other precious things. He found so much gold that he expected it to be more than two or even three horses could carry. He took all the gold and put it into two large chests and then took Grani by the bridle. The horse would not budge and whipping was useless. Sigurd now discovered what the horse wanted. He leapt onto his back and put spurs to him and the horse ran as if unencumbered.

## 21   CONCERNING SIGURD

Sigurd now rode a long way, until he came up on Hindarfell; then he turned south toward Frakkland.[63] Ahead of him on the mountain he saw a great light, as if a fire were burning and the brightness reached up to the heavens. And when he came to it, there stood before him a rampart of shields with a banner above it. Sigurd went into the rampart and saw a man lying there asleep, dressed in full armor. First he removed the helmet from the man's head and saw that it was a woman. She was in a coat of mail so tight that it seemed to have grown into her flesh.

He sliced through the armor, down from the neck opening and out through the sleeves, and it cut like cloth. Sigurd said she had slept too long. She asked what was so strong that it could slash through her coat of mail "and rouse me from sleep. Or is it that Sigurd the son of Sigmund has come, the one who has the helmet of Fafnir and carries Fafnir's bane in his hand?" Sigurd replied: "He is of the line of Volsung who has done this work. And I have heard that you are the daughter of a powerful king. I have also been told of your beauty and wisdom, and these I will put to the test."

Brynhild said that two kings had fought. One, called Hjalmgunnar, was old and was a great warrior, and Odin had promised him the victory. The other was Agnar or Audabrodir. "I struck down Hjalmgunnar in battle, and Odin stabbed me with a sleeping thorn in revenge. He said I should never afterward have the victory. He also said that I must marry. And I made a countervow that I would marry no one who knew fear." Sigurd said: "Teach me the ways of mighty things."

She answered: "You know them better than I. But gladly I will teach you, if there is anything I know that will please you about runes or other matters that concern all things. Let us drink together and may the gods grant us a fair day, that you may gain profit and renown from my wisdom, and that you will later remember what we speak of." Brynhild filled a goblet, gave it to Sigurd, and spoke:

6.    Beer I give you,
     Battlefield's ruler,[64]
     With strength blended
     And with much glory.

It is full of charmed verse
And runes of healing,
Of seemly spells
And of pleasing speech.[65]

7. Victory runes shall you know
If you want to secure wisdom,
And cut them on the sword hilt,
On the center ridge of the blade,
And the parts of the brand,
And name Tyr twice.[66]

8. Wave runes shall you make
If you desire to ward
Your sail-steeds[67] on the sound.
On the stem shall they be cut
And on the steering blade
And burn them on the oar.
No broad breaker will fall
Nor waves of blue,
And you will come safe from the sea.

9. Speech runes shall you know
If you want no repayment
In hate words for harm done.
Wind them,
Weave them,
Tie them all together,
At that *thing*[68]
When all shall attend
The complete court.

10. Ale runes shall you know
If you desire no other's wife
To deceive you in troth, if you trust.
They shall be cut on the horn
And on the hand's back
And mark the need rune on your nail.

11. For the cup shall you make a sign
And be wary of misfortune

And throw leek into the liquor.
Then, I know that,
You will never get
A potion blended with poison.

12. Aid runes shall you learn
If you would grant assistance
To bring the child from the mother.
Cut them in her palm
And hold her hand in yours.
And bid the Disir not to fail.

13. Branch runes shall you know
If you wish to be a healer
And to know how to see to wounds.
On bark shall they be cut
And on needles of the tree
Whose limbs lean to the east.

14. Mind runes shall you learn
If you would be
Wiser than all men.
They were solved,
They were carved out,
They were heeded by Hropt.[69]

15. They were cut on the shield
That stands before the shining god,
On Arvak's ear
And on Alsvid's head[70]
And on the wheel that stands
Under Hrungnir's chariot,[71]
On Sleipnir's reins,
And on the sleigh's fetters.

16. On bear's paw
And on Bragi's[72] tongue,
On wolf's claws
And on eagle's beak,
On bloody wings
And on bridge's ends,[73]

On the soothing palm
And on the healing step.

17. On glass and on gold
And on good silver,
In ale and in wine
And on the witch's seat,
In human flesh
And the point of Gaupnir[74]
And the hag's breast,
On the Norn's nail
And the neb of the owl.

18. All that were carved on these
Were scraped off
And mixed with the holy mead[75]
And sent on widespread ways.
They are with elves,
Some with the Æsir
And with the venerable Vanir,[76]
Some belong to mortal men.

19. These are cure runes[77]
And aid runes
And all ale runes
And peerless power runes
For all to use unspoiled
And unprofaned,
To bring about good fortune.
Enjoy them if you have learned them,
Until the gods perish.[78]

20. Now shall you choose,
As you are offered a choice,
O maple shaft of sharp weapons.[79]
Speech or silence,
You must muse for yourself.
All words are already decided.

Sigurd answered:

21. I will not flee, though
Death-fated you know I am,

I was not conceived as a coward.
I will have all
Of your loving advice
As long as I live.

## 22    Brynhild's Wise Counsel

Sigurd said: "Never can there be found a wiser woman in the world than you. Give me more wise counsel." Brynhild answered: "It is right to do your bidding and to give you good advice, because you seek it wisely." Then she said: "Do well by your kinsmen and take little revenge for their wrongdoings. Endure with patience and you will win long-lasting praise. Beware of ill dealings, both of a maid's love and a man's wife; ill often arises from these. Control your temper with foolish men at crowded gatherings, for they frequently speak worse than they know. When you are called a coward, people may think that you are rightfully named so. Kill the man another day, rewarding him for his malicious words.

"If you travel a road where evil creatures dwell, be wary. Although caught by nightfall, do not take shelter near the road, for foul beings who bewilder men often live there.

"Even if you see beautiful women at a feast, do not let them entice you so that they interfere with your sleep or distress your mind. Do not allure them with kisses and other tenderness. And if you hear foolish words from drunken men, do not dispute with those who are drunk on wine and have lost their wits. To many men such things bring much grief or even death.

"It is better to fight with your enemies than to be burned at home. And do not swear a false oath, because hard vengeance follows the breaking of truce. Do the right thing by dead men, be they dead from disease, by drowning, or by a weapon. Prepare their bodies with care. And do not trust any man, even though he is young, whose father or brother or close kinsman has been killed by you; often a wolf lies in a young son. Beware of the wiles of friends. I see only a little of your future life, yet it would be better if the hate of your in-laws did not descend upon you."

Sigurd said: "No one is wiser than you. And I swear that I shall marry you, for you are to my liking." She replied: "I would most

prefer to marry you, even should I choose from among all men."
And this they pledged with vows between them.

## 23    CONCERNING SIGURD'S APPEARANCE

Now Sigurd rode away. His ornamented shield was plated with red
gold and emblazoned with a dragon. Its top half was dark brown
and its bottom half light red, and his helmet, saddle, and buffcoat
were all marked in this way. He wore a mail coat of gold and all
his weapons were ornamented with gold. In this way the dragon
was illustrated on all his arms, so that when he was seen, all who
had heard the story would recognize him as the one who had killed
the great dragon called Fafnir by the Vaerings.[80] All Sigurd's
weapons were ornamented with gold and were brown in color since
he far surpassed other men in courtesy,[81] in noble bearing, and in
most other things. When all the mightiest champions and the most
famous chieftains are reckoned, he will always be counted the
foremost. His name is known in all tongues north of the Greek
Ocean, and so it must remain while the world endures.

Sigurd's hair was brown and splendid to see. It fell in long
locks. His beard, of the same color, was thick and short. His nose
was high and he had a broad, chiseled face. His eyes flashed so
piercingly that few dared look beneath his brow. His shoulders
were as broad as if one were looking at two men. His body was
well proportioned in height and size and in all respects most becoming. It is a mark of his great height that when he girded himself
with the sword Gram, which was seven spans long, and waded
through a field of full-grown rye, the tip of the sword's sheath
grazed the top of the standing grain. And his strength exceeded his
stature.

He well knew how to handle a sword, hurl a spear, cast a jave-
lin, hold a shield, bend a bow, and ride a horse. Sigurd had also
learned many courtesies in his youth. He was a wise man, knowing
events before they happened, and he understood the language of
birds. Because of these abilities, little took him by surprise. He
could speak at length, and with such eloquence, that when he took
it upon himself to press a matter, everybody agreed even before he
was finished speaking that no course other than the one he advo-

cated was possible. It was his pleasure to support his men, to test himself in great deeds, and to take booty from his enemies and give it to his friends. He did not lack in courage and he never knew fear.

## 24    SIGURD COMES TO HEIMIR

Sigurd now rode until he came to a large estate. A great chieftain named Heimir ruled over it. He was married to the sister of Brynhild, called Bekkhild,[82] because she had stayed at home and learned needlework and other feminine skills. But Brynhild took up helmet and mail coat and went to battle. Thus she was called Brynhild.[83] Heimir and Bekkhild had a son named Alsvid, the most courteous of men.

Outside, men were playing at their sports. But when they saw the man riding up to the dwellings, they called a halt to their game and marveled at him, for they had never seen his like. They went to meet him and received him well. Alsvid asked Sigurd to stay and receive from him whatever he wished. Sigurd accepted this offer. Preparations were made to serve him nobly. Four men lifted the gold from his horse and a fifth took care of him. There were many rare and precious treasures to be seen. The men thought it great entertainment to look at the mail coats, helmets, huge rings, marvelously large gold cups, and all kinds of weapons.

Sigurd remained there a long time in great honor. The news of his magnificent deed, that he had killed the terrible dragon, had now spread throughout all lands. The men enjoyed themselves well and each was loyal to the other. And to amuse themselves they prepared their weapons, making arrow shafts and hunting with their hawks.

## 25    THE CONVERSATION BETWEEN SIGURD AND BRYNHILD

Now Brynhild, Heimir's foster daughter, had come home. She stayed in a bower with her maidens. More skilled in handicraft than other women, she embroidered her tapestry with gold and on it stitched stories of the noble deeds that Sigurd had wrought: the slaying of the serpent, the seizing of the gold, and the death of Regin. It is said that one day Sigurd rode into the woods with his hounds and hawks and many followers. When he returned home, his hawk flew to a high tower and settled by a window. Sigurd went after the hawk. Then he saw a fair woman and realized that it was Brynhild. Both her beauty and her work affected him deeply. He went to the hall but did not want to join in the sport of the men. Then Alsvid said: "Why are you so quiet? This change in you concerns us, your friends. Why can you not be merry? Your hawks are moping, as is your horse Grani, and it will be a long time before this is amended."

Sigurd answered: "Good friend, listen to what is on my mind. My hawk flew to a tower and when I captured him, I saw a beautiful woman. She sat at a golden tapestry and embroidered there my past deeds." Alsvid replied: "You have seen Brynhild, the daughter of Budli, a woman of most noble bearing." Sigurd answered: "That must certainly be so. When did she get here?" Alsvid said: "There was only a short time between your arrivals." Sigurd said: "This I learned just a few days ago. This woman seemed to me the best in the world."

Alsvid spoke: "Such a man as you should not pay attention to a woman. It is bad to pine for what cannot be obtained." "I shall meet her," said Sigurd. "I shall give her gold and gain mutual affection and love." Alsvid answered: "There has yet to be a man that she allows to sit by her or to whom she gives ale to drink. She wants to go warring and win all kinds of fame." Sigurd said: "I do not know whether she will answer me or not or whether she will let me sit by her."

The next day Sigurd went to her chamber. Alsvid stood outside by the room, making arrow shafts. Sigurd said: "Be greeted, lady. And how do you fare?" She replied: "I am faring well. My kin and friends are alive, but it is unknown what fortune men will have to their dying day."

He sat down next to her. Then four women entered bearing large gold goblets and the best of wine and stood before them. Brynhild said: "That seat is granted to few, except when my father comes." Sigurd replied: "Now it is granted to whoever pleases me." The room was hung with the most precious tapestries and cloth covered the whole floor. Sigurd said: "Now it has happened as you promised me." She answered: "You will be welcomed here."

Then she rose up and the four maidens with her. She brought him a gold cup, and invited him to drink. He reached toward the cup but took her hand, drawing her down beside him. He put his arms around her neck and kissed her, saying: "No fairer woman than you has ever been born." Brynhild said: "It is wiser counsel not to put your trust in a woman, because women always break their promises."

Sigurd said: "The best day for us would be when we can enjoy each other." Brynhild said: "It is not fated that we should live together. I am a shield-maiden. I wear a helmet and ride with the warrior kings. I must support them, and I am not averse to fighting." Sigurd answered: "Our lives will be most fruitful if spent together. If we do not live together, the grief will be harder to endure than a sharp weapon."

Brynhild replied: "I must review the troops of warriors, and you will marry Gudrun, the daughter of Gjuki." Sigurd answered: "No king's daughter shall entice me. I am not of two minds in this, and I swear by the gods that I will marry you or no other woman." She spoke likewise. Sigurd thanked her for her words and gave her a gold ring. They swore their oaths anew. He went away to his men and was with them for a time, prospering greatly.

## 26    CONCERNING KING GJUKI AND HIS SONS

There was a king named Gjuki whose kingdom was south of the Rhine. He had three sons whose names were Gunnar, Hogni, and Guttorm.[84] Gudrun, his daughter, was the most famous of maidens. They surpassed the children of other kings both in looks and in stature, and in all their accomplishments. They were always harrying and performed many great feats. Gjuki was married to Grimhild, a woman well versed in magic.

There was a king named Budli. He was more powerful than Gjuki, although both of them were powerful. Atli[85] was the name of Brynhild's brother. He was a grim man, large and dark, yet he had a princely bearing and was an exceptional warrior. Grimhild was a grim-minded woman. The realm of the Gjukungs flourished, chiefly because of Gjuki's children, who surpassed most others in every way.

One time Gudrun told her maidens that she could not be happy. One woman asked her what was troubling her. She answered: "I do not prosper in my dreams, and my heart grieves because of this. Explain my dream since you inquire about it." "Tell me and do not be distressed," the woman replied, "because always one dreams before storms." Gudrun answered: "This dream has nothing to do with weather. I dreamt that I saw a handsome hawk on my hand. His feathers were of a golden hue." The woman replied: "Many have heard of your beauty, wisdom, and courtesy. Some king's son will ask for you in marriage." Gudrun continued. "I cared for nothing more than for this hawk, and I would rather have lost all my wealth than him." "The man you marry will be well bred, and you will love him deeply," replied the woman. Gudrun said: "It vexes me not to know who he is. I will visit Brynhild; she will know."

They adorned themselves with gold and with beautiful raiments and traveled with their maidens until they came to Brynhild's hall. This hall was ornamented with gold and stood on a precipice. And when their train was seen, Brynhild was told that many women were driving toward the fortress in gilded wagons. "That must be Gudrun, the daughter of Gjuki," she said. "I dreamt about her last night. Let us go to meet her. No women more beautiful come to visit us."

They went out to greet Gudrun and her women and received them well. They entered the splendid hall. The interior of the hall was decorated with paintings and tapestries and much adorned with silver. Cloths were spread beneath their feet and all waited upon them. They had all sorts of games. Gudrun was very quiet. Brynhild said: "Why can't you be merry? Don't be this way. Let us all amuse ourselves together by talking of powerful kings and their splendid deeds." "Let us do that," said Gudrun. "And who do you consider to have been the foremost of kings?" Brynhild replied: "Haki and Hagbard, the sons of Hamund.[86] They performed many famous feats in warfare."

Gudrun answered: "They were great and renowned. Yet Sigar

took their sister and burned another in her house, and they are slow at revenge. But why have you not mentioned my brothers, who are now considered the foremost of men?" Brynhild said: "That is all very well, but they have not yet been sufficiently tried. And I know of one who far exceeds them, and that is Sigurd, the son of King Sigmund. He was still a boy when he killed the sons of King Hunding and avenged his father and Eylimi, his mother's father." Gudrun said: "What is the proof of that? Are you saying that he was already born when his father fell?"

Brynhild answered: "His mother went to the battlefield and found the wounded King Sigmund. She offered to bind his wounds, but he declared himself too old to fight anymore. He told her to take comfort, that she would bear an extraordinary son. And this prophecy was the insight of a wise man. After the death of King Sigmund, she went with King Alf, and Sigurd was raised there with great honor. Every day he performed many valiant deeds, and he is the most excellent man in the world."

Gudrun said: "You have learned about him because of love. But I have come here to tell you my dreams, for they have brought me grave concern." Brynhild replied: "Do not let such things vex you. Stay with your kinsmen, all of whom wish to make you happy."

## 27   BRYNHILD INTERPRETS GUDRUN'S DREAM

"I dreamt," said Gudrun, "that many of us left my bower together and saw a huge stag. He far surpassed other deer. His hair was of gold. We all wanted to catch the stag, but I alone was able to do so. The stag seemed finer to me than anything else. But then you shot down the stag right in front of me. That was such a deep sorrow to me that I could hardly stand it. Then you gave me a wolf's cub. It spattered me with the blood of my brothers."

Brynhild replied: "I will tell you just what will happen. To you will come Sigurd, the man I have chosen for my husband. Grimhild will give him bewitched mead, which will bring us all to grief. You will marry him and quickly lose him. Then you will wed King Atli. You will lose your brothers, and then you will kill Atli." Gudrun

answered: "The grief of knowing such things overwhelms me."
And now she and her attendants departed and traveled home to
King Gjuki.

## 28     THE ALE OF FORGETFULNESS IS BLENDED FOR SIGURD

Sigurd now rode away with that mass of gold, leaving his companions in friendship. With all his armor and burden he rode Grani, traveling until he came to the hall of King Gjuki. He rode into the fortress. One of the king's men saw him and said: "I think that one of the gods is coming here. This man is all equipped in gold. His horse is far larger than others and his weaponry is exceptionally fine. He is far above other men, and he himself surpasses other men."

The king went out with his retainers and greeted the man, asking: "Who are you, who rides into the castle? No one dares do this without the permission of my sons." He responded: "I am called Sigurd and I am the son of King Sigmund." King Gjuki said: "Be welcome here with us and receive everything you desire."

Sigurd entered the hall. Everyone was short compared with him. They all served him, and he remained there in great favor. Sigurd, Gunnar, and Hogni all rode together, but Sigurd surpassed them in all accomplishments, although they were all mighty men.

Grimhild perceived how much Sigurd loved Brynhild and how often he mentioned her. She thought it would be more fortunate if he settled there and married the daughter of King Gjuki. She also saw that no one could equal Sigurd and realized the importance of his support. Besides, he had exceptional wealth, far exceeding what men had known before. The king treated him as he did his sons, and they esteemed him more than themselves.

One evening when they sat together drinking, the queen rose, went to Sigurd, and said to him: "It is a great joy for us that you are here and we wish to set all good things before you. Take the horn and drink." He accepted it and drank from it. She said: "King Gjuki shall be your father, and I your mother, while Gunnar and Hogni and all who swear the oath shall be your brothers. Then your equal will not be found." Sigurd received this well and because of that drink he could not remember Brynhild. He stayed there for a while.

And one time Grimhild went to King Gjuki, put her arms around his neck, and said: "The most valiant hero that can be found in the world has come here. There would be much support in him. Give him your daughter in marriage along with many riches and such power as he wants, and he might be able to find pleasure here." The king replied: "It is a rare thing to offer one's daughter, but there is more honor in offering her to him than in having others propose marriage."

One evening Gudrun served the drink. Sigurd noticed that she was a beautiful woman and most courtly in all things. Sigurd stayed there for five seasons[87] and they lived in friendship and fame. Then the kings now spoke among themselves. King Gjuki said: "You have done us much good, Sigurd, and you have greatly strengthened our state."

Gunnar spoke: "We want to do everything to encourage you to stay here a long time. We will offer a position of authority and our sister's hand, and no one else would receive those things even if he were to ask for them." Sigurd answered: "Be thanked for this honor. I shall accept."

They now swore a pact of brotherhood, as if they were brothers born of the same parents. A magnificent feast was prepared, lasting many days. Sigurd now wed Gudrun. There were all sorts of festivities and entertainments to be seen and each day's feasting proved better than the one before.

They now traveled widely throughout the lands, performing many splendid deeds and killing many kings' sons. No men worked such bold deeds as they did. They returned home with a huge store of booty. Sigurd gave Gudrun some of Fafnir's heart to eat and after this she was much grimmer and wiser than before. Their son was called Sigmund.

One day Grimhild went to her son Gunnar and said: "You are prospering in all matters except one, that you are unmarried. Ask for Brynhild in marriage. That would be the noblest match you could make. And Sigurd will ride with you." Gunnar answered: "Certainly she is beautiful and I am not unwilling." He told his father and brothers and Sigurd and they all encouraged him.

## 29    SIGURD RIDES THROUGH THE WAVERING FLAMES OF BRYNHILD, THE DAUGHTER OF BUDLI

Now they magnificently prepared for their journey. They rode over mountains and through valleys to King Budli. They presented their request of marriage. He was well disposed to the match, provided Brynhild did not refuse. He said she was so proud that she would marry only the man she wanted.

They rode now to Hlymdale. Heimir received them well. Gunnar told of his errand. Heimir said that the choice of a husband was Brynhild's. He said that her hall was a short distance away and that he believed she would want to marry only that man who rode through the blazing fire surrounding it.

They found the hall and the fire, and there they saw a golden-roofed fortress with fire burning around the outside. Gunnar rode Goti, and Hogni rode Holkvir. Gunnar spurred his horse toward the fire, but he shied away. Sigurd said: "Why are you drawing back, Gunnar?" He answered: "The horse does not want to leap this fire," and he asked Sigurd to lend him Grani.

"He is at your disposal," said Sigurd. Gunnar now rode at the fire, but Grani did not want to go. Thus Gunnar could not ride through the fire. Sigurd and Gunnar exchanged shapes, as Grimhild had taught them. Then Sigurd rode with Gram in his hand and on his feet he bound golden spurs. When he felt the spurs, Grani leapt forward toward the fire. There was a deafening roar as the fire swelled and the earth began to tremble. The flames rose to the heavens. No one had dared do this before. It was as if he rode into pitch-darkness. Then the fire subsided. Sigurd dismounted and went into the hall.

Thus it is said:

22.    The fire began to flare
        And the earth to shudder
        And high flames
        To heaven towered.
        Few of the king's men
        Had courage enough

To ride into the fire
Or to leap across it.

23.   Sigurd with his sword
     Spurred Grani on.
     The flames expired
     Before the prince,
     The fire all fell back
     Before the fame-hungry one.
     The harness was radiant
     Which Regin had owned.

And when Sigurd got past the flames, he found a beautiful dwelling and inside it sat Brynhild. She asked who this man was. He called himself Gunnar, the son of Gjuki, "and with the consent of your father and the agreement of your foster father, you are my intended wife, provided I ride your wavering flame and if you should so decide." "I hardly know how to respond," she said. Sigurd stood straight upon the floor, resting on the hilt of his sword, and said to Brynhild: "I shall pay a generous marriage settlement of gold and precious treasures in return for your hand."

She answered gravely from her seat, like a swan on a wave, in her mail coat, with her sword in her hand and her helmet on her head. "Gunnar," she said, "do not speak of such things to me, unless you surpass every other man and you will kill those who have asked for me in marriage, if you have the courage to do so. I was in battle with the king of Gardariki[88] and our weapons were stained with the blood of men, and this I still desire." He replied: "You have performed many splendid feats, but now call to mind your vow: that, if this fire were crossed, you would go with the man who did it." She recognized the truth in his answer and the significance of his speech. She rose and received him well.

He stayed there for three nights and they slept in one bed. He took the sword Gram and lay it unsheathed between them. She asked why he put it there. He said it was fated that he must celebrate his marriage in this manner or else die. He took from her the ring Andvaranaut, which he had given her, and gave her now another ring from Fafnir's inheritance. After this he rode away through the same fire to his companions. Sigurd and Gunnar changed back into their own shapes and then rode to Hlymdale and related what had passed.

That same day Brynhild journeyed home to her foster father. She told him in private that a king had come to her "and rode through my wavering flames, declaring he had come to win me. He called himself Gunnar. Yet when I swore the oath on the mountain, I had said that Sigurd alone could do that, and he is my first husband." Heimir said that it would have to remain as it was. Brynhild said: "My daughter by Sigurd, Aslaug,[89] shall be raised here with you."

The kings now went home, and Brynhild went to her father. Grimhild received them well and thanked Sigurd for his support. A feast was prepared and a great many people came. King Budli came with his daughter and his son Atli. And the feast lasted many days. When the celebration ended Sigurd remembered all his vows to Brynhild, although he did not let this be known. Brynhild and Gunnar sat together at the entertainment and drank good wine.

## 30    DISPUTE OF THE QUEENS, BRYNHILD AND GUDRUN

One day Brynhild and Gudrun went to bathe in the river Rhine. Then Brynhild waded farther out in the river. Gudrun asked what this meant. Brynhild said: "Why should I be your equal more in this than in other matters? I think my father is more powerful than yours, and my husband has accomplished many splendid feats and rode through the burning fire, but your husband was a thrall of King Hjalprek." Gudrun answered angrily: "It would be wiser for you to hold your tongue than to insult my husband. Everyone agrees that no one at all like him has come into the world. It is not fitting for you to insult him, because he was your first man. He killed Fafnir and rode the wavering flames when you thought it was King Gunnar. He lay with you and took from your hand the ring Andvaranaut, which you can now see here for yourself."

Brynhild saw the ring, recognized it, and became as pale as death. Brynhild went home and spoke no word that evening. When Sigurd came to bed Gudrun asked: "Why is Brynhild so gloomy?"

Sigurd replied: "I am not certain, but I suspect that we shall soon know more clearly." Gudrun said: "Why does she not take delight in wealth and happiness and in the praise of all men, as she married the man she wanted?" Sigurd said: "Where was she when she said this, that she thought herself to have the best man or the one that she most wanted to marry?" Gudrun answered: "In the morning I shall inquire whom she most wants to marry." "This I ask you not to do," Sigurd replied, "for once done, you will repent it."

That morning they sat in their bower, and Brynhild was silent. Then Gudrun said: "Be cheerful, Brynhild. Did our conversation distress you? What prevents your happiness?" Brynhild replied: "Malice alone brought you to this. You have a grim heart." "Do not think that," said Gudrun. "Tell me instead."

Brynhild answered: "Only ask what is best for you to know. That is suitable for noble women. And it is easy to be satisfied, while everything happens according to your desires." Gudrun replied: "It is early yet to boast, but this is somehow prophetic. Why are you goading me? I have done nothing to grieve you." "You shall pay for marrying Sigurd. I cannot bear that you enjoy him and that vast gold treasure," Brynhild answered. "I did not know of your agreement," said Gudrun, "and my father might well arrange a marriage for me without consulting you."

Brynhild replied: "Our talk was not secret and yet we had sworn oaths. You knew that you were betraying me. And that betrayal I shall avenge." Gudrun answered: "You are better married than you deserve. But your pride will not easily subside and many will pay for this." "I would have been content," said Brynhild, "if you did not have the nobler man." Gudrun answered: "You have such a noble husband with abundant wealth and power that it is uncertain who is the greater king." Brynhild replied: "Sigurd fought Fafnir and that is worth more than all of Gunnar's power," as is told:

24. Sigurd fought the dragon
    And that afterward will be
    Forgotten by no one
    While men still live.
    Yet your brother[90]
    Neither dared

> To ride into the fire
> Nor to leap across it.

Gudrun replied: "Grani would not run the fire with King Gunnar on him, but Gunnar dared to ride into it. There is no need to challenge his courage." "I do not hide my lack of goodwill for Grimhild," Brynhild said. Gudrun answered: "Do not blame her, for she treats you like her own daughter." Brynhild replied: "She contrived the whole onset of this misfortune that consumes us. She brought Sigurd the ruinous ale, so that he could not remember my name." Gudrun answered: "You speak many unjust words—it is a great lie."

Brynhild replied: "Enjoy Sigurd as if you had not betrayed me. You are undeserving to live together. May things proceed for you as I foresee." Gudrun answered: "I will enjoy more than you would wish. No one has reported that he was too good to me, not even once." Brynhild answered: "You are spiteful in your speech. When you regain your composure, you will regret this conversation. Let us no longer bandy words of hate." Gudrun said: "You first flung malicious words at me. Now you act in a conciliatory way, yet hatred is at the root of this."

"Let us stop this useless chatter," said Brynhild. "I kept my silence for a long time about the sorrow in my breast, yet I love only your brother. Let us speak of other things." Gudrun said: "Your thoughts see far beyond the present."

Great sorrow came to pass because they went to the river and Brynhild recognized the ring, from which their conversation arose.

## 31     BRYNHILD'S GRIEF ONLY INCREASES

After this conversation Brynhild took to her bed. King Gunnar received word that she was sick, and he went to see her, asking what vexed her. But she did not respond and lay as if dead. And when he persisted in the matter, she answered: "What did you do with the ring I gave you? King Budli gave me this ring at our last parting, when you, the sons of King Gjuki, came to him and swore you would destroy and burn if you did not get me. He then took me aside and asked which man of those who had come I would choose.

But I offered to defend the land and to be commander of a third of the army. There were then two choices at hand: either I would have to marry the man he wished or give up all wealth and his pledge of friendship. He said that his friendship was more profitable for me than his anger.

"Then I debated with myself whether I should submit to his will or kill many men. I thought myself powerless to contend with him. So it happened that I betrothed myself to the one who would ride the horse Grani with Fafnir's inheritance, to that one who would ride through my wavering flames and would kill those men who I decided should die. Now, no one dared to ride except Sigurd alone. He rode through the fire because he was not short of courage for the deed. He killed the dragon and Regin and five kings—unlike you, Gunnar, who blanched like a corpse. You are neither king nor champion. And I made this solemn vow at my father's home that I would love that man alone who is the noblest man born, and that is Sigurd. Now I am a breaker of oaths, as I do not have him. Because of this I shall bring about your death, and I have Grimhild to reward in an evil fashion. There is no woman worse or more cowardly."

Gunnar responded in such a manner that few heard: "You have spoken many false words, and you are a malicious woman to blame that woman who is far above you. She was not so discontent as you are, and she did not torment dead men.[91] She murdered no one and she is praised." Brynhild answered: "I have had no secret meetings, nor have I committed any crimes. My nature is different, and I might be more disposed to kill you." Then she wanted to kill King Gunnar, but Hogni put her in fetters. Gunnar then said: "I do not want her to live in chains."

Brynhild answered: "Do not concern yourself about that, because from this day on you will never see me cheerful in your hall. I will neither drink nor play chess, speak entertainingly, embroider fair garments with gold, nor give you advice." She declared it the most grievous sorrow that she was not married to Sigurd. She sat up and struck her tapestry so that it tore apart. She bid her chamber door be opened, so that her lamentations could be heard far away. Now the sorrow was boundless and was heard throughout the stronghold.

Gudrun asked her servingwomen why they were so gloomy

and sad: "What is wrong with you? Why do you go about like mad people? What panic has seized you?" Then a woman of the court, Svafrlod, answered: "This is an evil day. Our hall is full of grief."

Gudrun spoke to her friend: "Stand up, we have slept a long time. Wake Brynhild. We will go to our needlework[92] and be cheerful." "I will not do it," she said. "I will neither wake her nor speak to her. For many days she has drunk neither mead nor wine and a godlike wrath is upon her." Gudrun spoke to Gunnar: "Go visit her," she said, "and say that her grief pains us." Gunnar answered: "I am forbidden to see her or share her wealth."

Still Gunnar went to visit her and tried many directions of conversation with her, but he received nothing in the way of an answer. He went away now and met with Hogni, asking him to visit her. Hogni, though saying he was not eager to see her, went but got nothing from her. Then Sigurd was found and asked to visit her, but Sigurd did not reply. So matters stood that evening.

The next day, when Sigurd returned home from hunting, he met with Gudrun and said: "I have come to see that this horror is full of portent, and Brynhild will die." Gudrun answered: "My lord, strange and marvelous qualities are associated with her. She has now slept for seven days, so that none dare wake her." Sigurd replied: "She is not sleeping. She is plotting harsh deeds against us."

Then Gudrun spoke tearfully: "It is an enormous grief to foresee your death. Go rather and visit her and see whether her vehemence will subside. Give her gold and so appease her anger." Sigurd went out and found the hall open. He thought Brynhild asleep, drew back the bedcovers from her, and said: "Wake up, Brynhild. The sun is shining throughout the town, and you have slept enough. Throw off your sorrow and be happy." She said: "How arrogant you are to come to see me! No one has behaved worse toward me in this treachery."

Sigurd asked: "Why do you not speak to people? What is vexing you?" Brynhild answered: "I will tell you of my anger."

Sigurd said: "You are bewitched if you believe I think harshly of you. And you received as your husband the one you chose." "No," she said. "Gunnar did not ride through the fire to me, nor did he pay me the marriage settlement in slain men. I wondered at the man who entered my hall, and I thought I recognized your eyes, but I could not perceive clearly because of the veil that lay over my fate."

Sigurd said: "I am no nobler a man than the sons of Gjuki. They killed the king of the Danes and a great prince, the brother of King Budli." Brynhild answered: "I have many wrongs to discharge against them—do not remind me of my anguish. You, Sigurd, killed the serpent and rode through the fire for my sake. The sons of Gjuki did not do that." Sigurd answered: "I did not become your husband nor you my wife, and a noble king paid your marriage settlement." Brynhild replied: "I have never looked so upon Gunnar that my heart was gladdened. I loathe him, although I conceal it from others."

"It is terrible," said Sigurd, "not to love such a king. But what troubles you most? It seems to me that his love would be worth more than gold to you." Brynhild answered: "It is the most grievous of all my sorrows that I cannot bring it about that a sharp blade be reddened with your blood." Sigurd said: "Hold your judgment. It is a short wait until a biting sword will stick in my heart, and you could not ask for worse for yourself, because you will not live after me. From here on few days of life are left to us."

Brynhild answered: "Your words do not come from little distress, since you cheated me of all delight; I care not about my life." Sigurd replied: "Live, and love King Gunnar and me, and I will give all my treasure so that you do not die." Brynhild said: "You do not altogether know my character. You surpass all men, yet no woman has become more loathsome to you than I."

"Something else is closer to the truth," replied Sigurd. "I love you more than myself, although I was the object of the deceit that cannot now be changed. Always when my mind was my own,[93] it pained me that you were not my wife. But I bore it as well as I could since I lived in the king's hall. Yet I was happy that we were all together. It may be that what was earlier foretold will have to happen, but it shall not be feared." Brynhild answered: "You have delayed too long in telling me that my sorrow grieves you, and now I shall find no comfort." "I should like us both to enter one bed," said Sigurd, "and you to be my wife."

Brynhild answered: "Such things are not to be said. I will not have two kings in one hall. And sooner would I die before I would deceive King Gunnar." Now she recalled their meeting on the mountain and sworn oaths—"but now everything has changed and I do not want to live." "I could not remember your name," said Sigurd. "I did not recognize you until you were married. And that is my deepest sorrow."

Then Brynhild spoke: "I swore an oath to marry that man who would ride through my wavering flames, and that oath I would hold to or else die." "Rather than have you die, I will forsake Gudrun and marry you," said Sigurd. And his sides swelled so that the links of his mail burst. "I do not want you," said Brynhild, "or anyone else." Sigurd went away.

As it is told in the "Lay of Sigurd,"

25.  Out went Sigurd
     Leaving talk,
     Heroes' worthy friend,
     And grieved so deeply
     That the heaving breast
     Of the battle-eager one
     Sheared from his sides
     The iron-woven shirt.

And when Sigurd entered the hall, Gunnar asked if he knew what Brynhild's affliction was and whether she had recovered her speech. Sigurd said she was able to speak. And now Gunnar went to visit her again and asked what her sorrow meant and whether there was a cure for it. "I do not want to live," said Brynhild, "because Sigurd has betrayed me, and he betrayed you no less, when you let him come into my bed. Now I do not want to have two husbands at the same time in one hall. This shall be Sigurd's death or yours or mine, because he has told Gudrun everything, and she reviles me."

## 32    THE BETRAYAL OF SIGURD

After this Brynhild went out and sat under her chamber wall. She lamented grievously, declaring everything, both land and power, hateful to her, since she did not have Sigurd. And Gunnar came to her again. Then Brynhild said: "You shall lose both power and wealth, life and me, and I shall journey home to my kin and remain there in sorrow unless you kill Sigurd and his son. Do not raise the wolf cub."

Gunnar now became very distressed. He thought he did not know the best course to pursue, for he was bound by oath to Sigurd. And various thoughts shifted in his mind, but he thought the worst dishonor would be if his wife left him. Gunnar said: "Brynhild is more precious to me than anything else, and she is the most renowned of all women. I would forfeit my life rather than lose her love."

And he called his brother Hogni to him and said: "I am confronted with a difficult choice." He said that he wanted to kill Sigurd, that Sigurd had betrayed his trust: "We will then also control the gold and have all the power." Hogni said: "It is not fitting for us to violate our oaths by breaching the peace. And we have had much support from him. No kings are our equal as long as this king of Hunland lives. And we will never get such a brother-in-law again. Consider how valuable it would be for us to have such a brother-in-law and nephews, too. But I see how this problem arose. Brynhild stirred it up, and her advice will lead us to disgrace and destruction."

Gunnar answered: "We will make this event come about, and I see the means. Let us urge our brother Guttorm to act. He is young, knows little, and is not bound by any oath." Hogni said: "That seems poor advice to me. And even if the deed is done, we will pay for betraying such a man." Gunnar said Sigurd must die, "or else I will die." He bid Brynhild rise and be cheerful. She stood up and said, however, that Gunnar would not enter into the same bed with her until this came about.

Now the two brothers talked together. Gunnar said it is a valid felony punishable by death for having taken Brynhild's maidenhead, "and let us urge Guttorm on to this deed." They called him to them and offered him gold and great power to perform the act. They took a snake and the flesh of a wolf and cooked them and gave this to him to eat, as the skald says:

26.   Some took wood-fish,[94]
     Some sliced a wolf's carrion,
     Some gave to Guttorm

The Wolf's[95] flesh
Mixed with ale.

They used these and many other kinds of witchcraft. And with this nourishment and Grimhild's persuasions and everything else, Guttorm became so violent and fierce that he promised to do the deed. They promised him great honor in return. Sigurd did not expect such deceit. He could also not prevail against either his fate or his death. Sigurd also did not perceive that he was deserving of betrayal from them.

Guttorm went into Sigurd's room the next morning, while he was resting in his bed. But when he looked at him, Guttorm did not dare attack and turned back to leave the room. And so it happened a second time. Sigurd's eyes flashed so sharply that few dared meet their gaze. But the third time he went in, Sigurd was asleep. Guttorm drew his sword and struck at Sigurd so that the blade stuck in the bed beneath him. Sigurd woke up from the wound, as Guttorm was leaving by the door. Sigurd then took the sword Gram and cast it after Guttorm. It struck him in the back and cut him into two at the waist. His lower body fell one way and his head and arms fell back into the room.

Gudrun was asleep in Sigurd's arms, but she awoke to unspeakable grief, drenched in his blood. She wailed so with tears and lamentations that Sigurd rose up on the pillow and spoke. "Do not weep," he said. "Your brothers live on to grant your pleasure. But I have a son too young to keep a watch out for his enemies, and they have provided poorly for themselves. They will not again find such a brother-in-law to ride with them in the army, or such a nephew, if he is allowed to grow up. And now it has come to pass as has long been foretold. I refused to believe it, but no one can withstand his fate. Brynhild, who loved me more than she did any other man, caused this betrayal. I will swear this, that I never did a disservice to Gunnar. I respected our oaths and I was never overly friendly with his wife. If I had known earlier what was going to happen and had risen to my feet, bearing my weapons, many would have lost their lives before I had fallen. All the brothers would have been slain. It would have been more difficult for them to kill me than the fiercest wild bison or boar."

The king now died. Gudrun let out a tormented moan. Brynhild heard it and laughed when she heard Gudrun sobbing. Then Gunnar said: "You do not laugh because you are happy in the depths of your heart. Or why has your color left you? You are a vile monster and most likely you are fated to die. No one would be more deserving than you to see King Atli killed before your eyes and to be forced to watch while it happened. We must now sit over our brother-in-law, the killer of our brother."

She replied: "No one will protest that there has been too little killing. But King Atli does not care about your threats or your anger. He will outlive you and be mightier." Hogni said: "Now it has come about, as Brynhild foresaw, and we will never remedy this evil deed." Gudrun said: "My relatives have killed my husband. Now you must ride at the head of the army, and when you come to battle, then you will find that Sigurd is no longer at your side. And you will then realize that Sigurd was your luck and your strength. If he had had sons such as himself, then you might have fortified yourself with his offspring and their kin."

Now no one thought himself capable of understanding why Brynhild had requested with laughter the deed that she now lamented with tears. Then she said: "I dreamt, Gunnar, that I had a cold bed and you were riding into the hands of your enemies. Your whole family will suffer an ill fate, for you are breakers of oaths. When you plotted his death, you did not clearly remember when you and Sigurd had mixed your blood together. You have rewarded him poorly for everything that he did in good faith for you and for letting you be the foremost. And when he came to me, his oaths were put to the test, for he lay his sharp-edged sword, tempered in venom, between us. But soon you plotted to harm him and me when I was at home with my father and had everything that I wanted. I did not intend that any of you would become my husband when you three kings rode toward the fortress. Then Atli took me aside and asked if I would marry the man who rode Grani. That one did not look like you. And then I promised myself to the son of King Sigmund and to no other. But things will not go well for you, even though I die."

Then Gunnar rose up and put his arms around her neck and begged her to live and to accept compensation. And all the others tried to dissuade her from dying. But she pushed away everyone who came to her, saying it was useless to try to keep her from what she intended to do. Then Gunnar appealed to Hogni, asking him for counsel. He begged Hogni to go and attempt to soften her temper, saying there was now a great need to allay her sorrow until time had passed. Hogni replied: "No man should hinder her dying, for she has never been any good to us or to any man since she came here."

Brynhild asked for a large amount of gold to be brought and requested all who wanted to accept a gift of wealth to come forward. Then she took a sword and stabbed herself under the arm, sank back into the pillows, and said: "Let each one who wants to receive gold take it now." They were all silent. Brynhild said: "Accept the gold and use it well."

Brynhild then spoke to Gunnar: "Now I will quickly tell you what will happen in the future. Through the counsels of Grimhild the sorceress, you will soon be reconciled with Gudrun. The daughter of Gudrun and Sigurd will be called Svanhild, and she will be the fairest of all women born. Gudrun will marry Atli against her will. You will want to have Oddrun,[96] but Atli will forbid it. You and Oddrun will then meet secretly and she will love you. Atli will betray you and put you in a snake pit, and then Atli and his sons will be killed; Gudrun will slay them. After that happens, huge waves will carry Gudrun to the fortress of King Jonakr, where she will give birth to noble sons. Svanhild will be sent out of the land and be married to King Jormunrek. The counsels of Bikki will sting her. With this all your race will be dead and gone and Gudrun's sorrows will be multiplied."

## 33    BRYNHILD'S REQUEST

Brynhild continued: "Now, Gunnar, I ask a final request of you: let one huge funeral pyre be raised on the level field for all of us: for me and Sigurd and for those who were killed with him. Let there be tents reddened with the blood of men. Burn the Hunnish king there at my side, and at his other side my men, two at his head, two at his feet, and two hawks. Thus it will be equally divided. Lay there between us a drawn sword, as before, when we entered one bed and vowed to become man and wife. The door will not close on his heels if I follow him, and our funerary procession[97] will not be unworthy if, following him, are five bondwomen and eight attendants given me by my father. And those who were killed with Sigurd will also burn there. I would speak further if I were not wounded, but now the gash hisses[98] and the wound is opening. But I have told the truth."

Sigurd's body was then prepared according to the ancient custom and a tall pyre was built. When it was fully kindled, the body of Sigurd, the bane of Fafnir, was laid on top of it, along with his three-year-old son, whom Brynhild had ordered killed, and the body of Guttorm. When the pyre was all ablaze, Brynhild went out upon it and told her chambermaids to take the gold that she wanted them to have. Then Brynhild died and her body burned there with Sigurd. Thus their lives ended.

## 34 THE DISAPPEARANCE OF GUDRUN

Everyone who now heard the news said that no man of Sigurd's like remained in the world, and never again would a man be born equal to Sigurd in all things. His name would never be forgotten in the German tongue and in the northern lands, as long as the world endures.

It is told that one day, while sitting in her chamber, Gudrun said: "My life was better when Sigurd was mine. He surpassed all men as gold does iron, the leek other herbs, and the stag other animals, until my brothers begrudged me such a man, the foremost of all. They could not sleep until they had killed him. Grani made a great din when he saw his wounded master. Later I spoke with him as if he were a man, but his head dropped toward the earth and he knew that Sigurd had fallen."

Then Gudrun disappeared into the forest.[99] All about her she heard the cries of wolves, and she thought it would be more agreeable to die than to live. Gudrun journeyed until she came to the hall of King Half. She stayed there in Denmark with Thora, the daughter of Hakon, for seven half years, and she was treated with generous hospitality. Gudrun wove a tapestry on which she depicted many great deeds as well as fair games, which were common in those days. It also showed swords and mail coats and all the trappings of a king, as well as the ships of King Sigmund, sailing off the coast. Gudrun and Thora embroidered the battle of Sigar and Siggeir at Fjon in the south. Such was their entertainment, and Gudrun was now somewhat comforted in her sorrow.

Grimhild, finding out where Gudrun had settled, summoned her sons to speak with her. She asked them how they wanted to compensate Gudrun for her son and her husband, and said they were obligated to do so. Gunnar spoke, declaring that he would give her gold to recompense her for her grief. They summoned their friends, readied their horses, and prepared their helmets, shields, swords, coats of mail, and all kinds of armor. The expedition was outfitted most splendidly, and no champion of merit stayed at home. The horses were armored and every knight had either a gilded or a brightly polished helmet. Grimhild decided to join them on their journey, saying that their errand would be completed only if she did not stay at home. In all there were five hundred men, among them men of renown: Valdamar of Denmark and Eymod and Jarisleif. They entered King Half's hall. There were Langobards, Franks, and Saxons. They traveled in full armor and wore red fur cloaks, as is told:

27. Short mail coats,
    Molded helmets,
    Swords girded,
    Their hair cut short and brown.

They wanted to select fine gifts for their sister, and they spoke well to her. Yet, she trusted none of them. Then Grimhild brought Gudrun an evil potion which she was made to accept, and afterward she remembered none of her grievances. The drink was mixed with the strength of the earth and the sea and the blood of her son,[100] while the inside of the drinking horn was carved with all manner of runes, reddened with blood, as is here told:

28. The horn was lined
    With runes manifold,
    Carved and cut with blood.
    Conceive them I could not:
    The long ling-fish[101]
    Of the Haddings' land,[102]
    Ears of corn uncut,[103]
    Entrails of beasts.[104]

29. In that ale were
    Evils aplenty:
    Herbs of all trees
    And acorn burned,
    Hearth's black dewfall,
    Entrails offered,
    Boar's liver boiled,
    So that blunted were claims.

After that, when their desires were in accord, there was great rejoicing. When she met Gudrun, Grimhild said: "Good fortune to you, daughter. I give you gold and all kinds of treasure from your father's legacy, precious rings and bed hangings of the most gracious Hunnish maids. Thus you will be compensated for your husband. Then you will be given in marriage to King Atli the Powerful. You will rule over his wealth. But do not abandon your kinsmen for the sake of one man; instead, you must do as we ask." Gudrun answered: "I will never marry King Atli. There is for us no honor in augmenting our kin through such a union."

Grimhild replied: "You must not now plan revenge. If you have sons, behave as if Sigurd and Sigmund were alive." Gudrun said: "Never will Sigurd be far from my thoughts, for he was best among men." Grimhild insisted: "You are ordered to marry King Atli, or you shall not marry at all." Gudrun answered her: "Do not offer me this king, for from my marriage with him only grief for our family will arise. He will treat your sons cruelly and afterward grim vengeance will fall upon him." Grimhild, disturbed by Gudrun's statements about her sons, said: "Do as we ask and you will receive great honor and our friendship, as well as the regions that go by the names of Vinbjorg and Valbjorg." Grimhild's words carried such weight that this had to come about. Gudrun said: "This must happen then, although it be against my will. And it will lead to little joy. Rather, it will bring grief."

They all then mounted their horses and their women were put in wagons. They traveled for seven days by horse, another seven by ship, and the third seven again over land, until they came to a high palace. A large number of people came to greet Gudrun and a splendid feast was prepared, as had earlier been agreed between them. The banquet proceeded with honor and magnificence. At this feast Atli drank the marriage toast to Gudrun. But her thoughts never laughed with him, and their life together contained little affection.

## 35   GUDRUN CARVES RUNES

Now it is said that on a certain night King Atli awoke from his sleep. He spoke with Gudrun. "I dreamt," he said, "that you thrust at me with a sword." Gudrun interpreted the dream, saying that to dream of iron indicated fire and "your self-deception in thinking yourself the foremost of all."

Atli then said: "I dreamt further. It seemed to me that two reeds were growing here and I wanted never to harm them. Then they were torn up by the roots and reddened with blood, brought to the table, and offered to me to eat. I then dreamt that two hawks flew from my hand, that they had no prey to catch, and thus went down to Hel. It seemed to me that their hearts were mixed with honey and that I ate of them. Afterward it seemed to me that handsome whelps lay before me and cried out loudly, and I ate their corpses unwillingly." Gudrun said: "Your dreams do not bode well, yet they will be fulfilled. Your sons are fated to die and many oppressive events are in store for us." "Furthermore I dreamt," he said, "that I lay bedridden and that my death had been contrived."

Now time passed and their life together was cold. King Atli pondered the whereabouts of the hoard of gold that Sigurd had owned, but of which only King Gunnar and his brother now knew. Atli was a great and powerful king; he was wise and had a large following. He took counsel with his men as to which course of action should be followed. He knew that Gunnar and his kin had more wealth than anyone else. He now resolved to send men to meet the brothers, invite them to a banquet, and honor them in many ways. A man called Vingi led King Atli's messengers.

The queen, aware of the king's private meeting with his counselors, suspected there would be treachery toward her brothers. Gudrun cut runes, and took a gold ring and tied a wolf's hair onto it. She gave it to the king's messengers who then departed as the king had ordered. Before they stepped ashore, Vingi saw the runes and changed them in such a way that Gudrun appeared to be urging the brothers to come and meet with Atli. Then they arrived at King

Gunnar's hall; they were received well and large fires were built for them. They drank the finest drink with good cheer. Then Vingi said: "King Atli sent me here to ask you to visit him in great honor and to receive great honor from him, as well as helmets and shields, swords and mail coats, gold and fine clothes, troops and horses, and a large fief. He declares it best that you succeed him."

Gunnar turned aside and asked Hogni: "What shall we make of this offer? He is asking us to accept vast power, yet I know of no kings with as much gold as we have, because we have all the gold that lay on Gnitaheath. We have large chambers filled with gold and with the best of edged weapons and all kinds of armor. I know my horse to be the finest and my sword the sharpest, the gold the most precious." Hogni answered: "I wonder at his offer, for it is not like him to behave in this way. It seems inadvisable to go to visit him. And when I looked at the treasures King Atli had sent us, I wondered at the wolf's hair I saw tied around a gold ring. It may be that Gudrun thinks he has the thoughts of a wolf toward us, and that she does not want us to go." Vingi then showed him the runes that he said Gudrun had sent them.

Now most people went to sleep, but some stayed up drinking with a few of the men. Hogni's wife, Kostbera, the fairest of women, went and looked at the runes. Gunnar's wife, named Glaumvor, was a woman of noble character. She and Kostbera served the drink, and the kings became very drunk. Vingi, observing their condition, said: "It cannot be concealed that King Atli is too old and too infirm to defend his kingdom, and his sons are too young and unprepared. Atli wants to give you authority over his kingdom while they are so young. He would be most contented if you made use of it." It happened that Gunnar by this time was very drunk and was being offered much power. He could also not escape his destiny. He vowed to make the journey and told his brother Hogni. Hogni replied: "Your word must stand and I will follow you, but I am not eager to make this trip."

When the men had drunk as much as they cared to, they went to bed. Kostbera began to look at the runes and to read the letters. She saw that something else had been cut over what lay underneath and that the runes had been falsified. Still she discerned through her wisdom what the runes said. After that she went to bed beside her husband. When they awoke she said to Hogni: "You intend to go away from home but that is inadvisable. Go instead another time. You cannot be very skilled at reading runes if you think your sister has asked you to come at this time. I read the runes and wondered how so wise a woman could have carved them so confusedly. Yet it seems that your death is indicated underneath. Either Gudrun missed a letter or someone else has falsified the runes. And now you shall hear my dream."

## 36    HOGNI INTERPRETS HIS WIFE'S DREAM

"In my dream it seemed as if a turbulent river had rushed in here and broken up the beams in the hall." Hogni replied: "You often have premonitions of evil, but it is not my nature to show hostility toward men unless it is deserved. Atli will receive us well."

She said: "You may put it to the test, yet friendship is not behind this invitation. I dreamt again that another river rushed through here with a terrible uproar. It demolished all the benches in the hall, and broke the legs of you and your brother both. That must signify something." "Crop fields must stretch out there where you thought there was a river," he replied. "When we walk through a field the large husks often cover our legs."

"I dreamt," she said, "that your bedcovers were ablaze, and that the fire leapt up from the hall." He answered: "I know quite clearly what that is. Our clothes are lying about neglected, and they are what will burn when your thoughts turn to bedcovers."

"I thought a bear entered here," she said. "He destroyed the king's throne and waved his paws so much about that we all grew afraid. He had us all in his mouth together, so that we could do nothing and great terror arose." He answered: "A strong tempest will come, where you thought it a white bear."

"I thought an eagle entered here and flew through the hall," she said, "splashing me, and all of us, with blood. That must bode ill, for it seemed to me that the eagle was the apparition of King Atli." He answered: "We often slaughter generously and kill large oxen for our pleasure. It signifies cattle when one dreams of an eagle. Atli means well by us." Thus they ended their talk.

## 37    The Brothers' Journey
from Home

It is told of Gunnar that the same thing happened when he and his wife awoke. Glaumvor, Gunnar's wife, spoke of her many dreams which seemed to her to portend betrayal, but Gunnar gave them all a different meaning.

"This was one of my dreams," she said, "I thought a bloody sword was carried here into the hall. You were pierced through with this sword, and wolves were howling at both ends of the sword." The king answered: "Little dogs will want to bite me there. The barking of dogs is often indicated by bloodied weapons."

She said: "Again I thought that somber-looking women entered here and chose you as husband. It could be that they were your *disir*."[105] He answered: "Things are becoming difficult to interpret, but no one can avoid death. It is not unlikely that I will be short-lived."

In the morning the men leapt up and wanted to leave, but others tried to dissuade them. Then Gunnar spoke to a man named Fjornir: "Get up and give us good wine to drink from large goblets, for it may be that this will be our last banquet. The old wolf will now get to the gold if we die, and the bear will not hesitate to bite with his battle-teeth." Then the weeping household led them out. Hogni's son said: "Farewell and enjoy good fortune."

Most of their warriors remained behind. Solar and Snaevar, the sons of Hogni, went with them, as well as a famous champion called Orkning, the brother of Bera.[106] The people followed them to the ships and everyone tried to persuade them not to go, but it was to no avail. Then Glaumvor spoke. "Vingi," she said, "it is very likely that serious misfortune will arise from your coming here and that significant events will arise from your journey." He replied: "I swear I am not lying. May the high gallows and all the demons take me if I lie with any word." He did not spare himself in such speeches. Then Bera said: "Farewell, and may good fortune be with you." "Be of good cheer, whatever happens to us," replied Hogni. They parted there, each with his own destiny.

They rowed so hard and with so much strength that almost half the keel came loose from the ship. They hauled hard on the oars with long pulls, so that the handles and oar pins broke. And when they made land they did not secure their ships. Then for a time they rode their excellent mounts through a dark forest. Finally they saw the king's dwelling. From there they heard a harsh clamor and the clash of arms. They saw a host of men and the many preparations they were making. At all the gates of the fortress there were crowds of men. The travelers rode up to the fortress but found it closed. Hogni broke open the gate and they rode into the stronghold. Then Vingi said: "You would better have left that undone. Now wait here while I look for a gallows tree for you. I asked you courteously to come here, but deceit lurked underneath. Now it will be only a short wait before you will be swinging aloft." Hogni answered: "We will not give way to you, and I doubt we will shrink back if this comes to a battle. It is of no use for you to try to frighten us—it will prove ill for you." Then they threw Vingi down and beat him to death with the blunt ends of their axes.

## 38 THE BATTLE IN THE FORTRESS AND THE VICTORY

They now rode to the king's hall. King Atli arranged his forces for battle; the formations were deployed so that a courtyard lay between them. "Be welcome here with us," he said, "and give me the store of gold that belongs to me, the treasure that Sigurd possessed and Gudrun now owns." Gunnar said: "You will never get that treasure and, if you offer us hostility, you will come up against resolute men before we give up our lives. It may be that you will provide, with magnificence and with little stinginess, a feast for the eagle and the wolf." "For a long time," replied Atli, "I have intended to take your lives, to control the gold, and to repay you for your villainy when you betrayed your finest brother-in-law. And I shall avenge him." Hogni answered: "It is of no help to you to have plotted this deed for a long time, for you are not ready."

A fierce battle then broke out, beginning with a shower of missiles. The news of the fighting came to Gudrun. When she heard it, she grew heavy with anger and sorrow. She threw off her cloak and then went out. She greeted those who had come, kissing her brothers and showing them affection. This was their last greeting.

She said: "I thought I had contrived a way to prevent your coming here. But no one can withstand his fate." And she added: "Is there any use in seeking a settlement?" But they all flatly refused.

Gudrun, seeing that the game was going against her brothers, set a bold course. She put on a mail coat, took up a sword, and fought beside her brothers, advancing like the most valiant of men. Everybody agreed that a stronger defense could hardly have been seen. A large number of men fell, yet the brothers' courage still surpassed that of others. The battle raged for a long time, right up to the middle of the day. Gunnar and Hogni went through King Atli's ranks, and it is said that the whole field was awash with blood. Hogni's sons pressed strongly forward. King Atli said: "I had a large splendid army and proud champions, yet now many of us have fallen and we have ill to repay you. Nineteen of my champions have been killed, and only eleven remain."

There was a pause in the fighting. Then King Atli said: "We were four brothers and now I am the only one left. I attached myself to a powerful family through a good marriage, thinking to further myself. I had a wise and beautiful wife, m̄agnanimous and determined, but I could not benefit from her wisdom, for we seldom agreed. Now you have killed many of my relatives, cheated me of treasure and kingdom, and contrived my sister's death, which grieves me the most." Hogni replied: "Why do you say such things? You broke the peace first. You took my kinswoman, starved her to death, murdered her, and took the treasure. Such conduct was not kingly, and I think it laughable that you are recounting your woes. I thank the gods that things are going badly for you."

## *39*   HOGNI IS CAPTURED

Now King Atli urged his troops to make a fierce assault. They fought valiantly, but the Gjukungs pressed forward so resolutely that King Atli was driven back into the hall. Now they fought inside and the battle raged savagely. There was heavy loss of life and the battle ended with the brothers' whole army fallen. Gunnar and Hogni were the only two left standing. Before that many a man was sent to Hel by their weapons. King Gunnar was now attacked and by dint of their superior strength, Atli's men seized and fettered him. Then Hogni fought on gallantly and courageously, killing twenty of King Atli's greatest champions. He flung many into the fire that had been built there in the hall. All were agreed that such a man had hardly ever been seen before. Nevertheless, at the end Hogni was overpowered and made prisoner. King Atli said: "It is astonishing how many men have fallen before him. Now, cut out his heart and may that be his death."

Hogni said: "Do as you like. I will gladly await whatever you choose to do. You will see that my heart is not timid and that I have encountered severe ordeals before. When I was not wounded, I willingly endured trials of adversity. But now I am sorely wounded, and you alone will decide our dispute." A counselor of King Atli's then spoke: "I have a better idea. Let us take instead the thrall Hjalli and spare Hogni. The thrall is destined for death; as long as he lives he will be trouble."

The thrall, hearing what was said, cried loudly and ran away to wherever he saw hope of shelter. He said he had drawn a bad lot from their enmity and he was the one to pay. He declared it would be an evil day when he would die and leave his soft life and his pig keeping. The men grabbed him and drew their knives out. He cried out loudly even before he felt the point. Then Hogni spoke, in a way that is customary for the strong when in deadly peril: he interceded for the thrall's life, saying he did not want to hear the shrieking, that this game was easier for himself to play. The thrall was then set free and granted his life.

Both Gunnar and Hogni were put in fetters. King Atli said to King Gunnar that he must tell him the location of the gold if he wanted to keep his life. Gunnar replied: "I would sooner see the bloody heart of my brother Hogni." They seized the thrall a second time, cut out his heart, and carried it to King Gunnar. He said: "Here can be seen the heart of Hjalli the cowardly; it is unlike the heart of Hogni the valiant, for it quakes tremulously. Yet it quaked even more when it lay in his breast."

Now, at the urging of King Atli, they seized Hogni and cut out his heart. Hogni's strength was so immense that he laughed while he suffered this torture. Everyone wondered at his courage and it has been remembered ever since. They showed Gunnar the heart of Hogni. Gunnar answered: "Here now can be seen the heart of Hogni the valiant; it is unlike the heart of Hjalli the cowardly, because it stirs little. Yet it stirred still less when it lay in his breast. So, Atli, you will lose your life as we now lose ours. I alone now know where the gold is, and Hogni cannot tell you. My mind wavered while we both lived, but now I alone have the decision. Rather shall the Rhine rule over the gold than the Huns wear it on their arms." King Atli said: "Take the prisoner away." And it was done.

Gudrun now summoned men to her, met with Atli, and said: "May misfortune go with you now, in the same measure as you kept your word to Gunnar and me." King Gunnar was then placed in a snake pit with many serpents, and his hands were bound fast. Gudrun sent him a harp and he showed his skill by artfully plucking the strings with his toes. He played so exceedingly well that few thought they had heard such strumming even with the hands. And he continued playing skillfully until all the serpents had fallen asleep, except for one large and hideous adder which crawled up to him and burrowed with its head until it struck his heart. And there, with much valor, Gunnar lost his life.

## 40 THE CONVERSATION BETWEEN ATLI AND GUDRUN

King Atli now thought that he had won a great victory. He told Gudrun about it in a mocking tone, or as if he were bragging: "Gudrun," he said, "now you have lost your brothers, and you yourself brought it about." She answered: "You delight in announcing these killings to me, but you may regret what happened when you experience what follows. The legacy that will endure the longest is undying cruelty. Things will never go well for you while I live."

Atli replied: "We two should now make our peace. I will recompense you for the death of your brothers with gold and precious gifts, according to your desire." "For a long time I have not been easy to deal with," she said, "but I could tolerate matters while Hogni lived. You will never pay for my brothers to my satisfaction. Yet we women are often forced to bow to your strength. My kinsmen are now all dead and you alone have control over me. I shall accept my lot. Let us prepare a great feast—I will thus honor my brothers and your kin." She spoke now with gentle words, although underneath she was no less afflicted. When she made herself speak so mildly, he was swayed and believed her words to be sincere.

Gudrun prepared a funeral feast for her brothers and King Atli did the same for his men. And it was a turbulent feast. Gudrun thought about her sorrows and waited for a chance to bestow some profound dishonor upon the king. In the evening she seized the sons she had by King Atli as they played beside their bedposts. The boys became downcast and asked what they were supposed to do. "Do not ask," she replied. "Both of you will be killed." "You may do with your children as you like," said the boys. "No one will hinder you, but there will be shame for you in this act." Then she slit their throats.

The king asked where his sons were. Gudrun replied: "I will tell you and gladden your heart. You caused me heavy sorrow when you killed my brothers. Now you shall hear what I have to tell you. You have lost your sons—on the table both their skulls are serving as cups—and you yourself drank their blood mixed with wine. Then I took their hearts and roasted them on a spit, and you ate them."

King Atli answered: "Cruel you are to murder your sons and give me their flesh to eat. Little time is lost between your wicked deeds." Gudrun said: "It is my desire to bring grievous shame upon you. No punishment can ever be cruel enough for such a king." The king spoke: "Your monstrous deed is unparalleled in the memories of men. There is much lack of wisdom in such brutality. It is fitting for you to be stoned to death and burned on a pyre. Thus you would get what you deserve from choosing this path." She replied: "You prophesy this for yourself, but I will be allotted a different death." They exchanged many malicious words.

Hogni had left behind a son named Niflung.[107] He bore a profound hatred toward King Atli and told Gudrun that he wanted to avenge his father. She welcomed this idea, and together they conceived their plans. Gudrun said it would be a lucky deed if vengeance could be done. In the evening, when the king had drunk, he went to bed. When he was asleep Gudrun and the son of Hogni came. Gudrun took a sword and thrust it into King Atli's chest. Both Gudrun and Hogni's son worked the deed together.

King Atli awoke at the wound and said: "There is no need for bandages or for cures. But who inflicted this wound on me?" Gudrun said: "I had a part in it, as did the son of Hogni." King Atli said: "It was not honorable for you to do this, although there was some cause for it. You were married to me at your relatives' counsel and I paid a marriage settlement for you of thirty good knights and comely maidens and many other men. Yet you would not comport yourself with moderation unless you controlled the lands that King Budli had possessed, and you often caused your mother-in-law to shed tears."

Gudrun said: "You have spoken much that is untrue, but I do not care about that. I was frequently harsh-tempered, yet you made my temper much worse. There has often been much contention here in your court. Your relatives and your friends often fought and each baited the other. Life was better when I was with Sigurd. We slew kings and ruled over their territories, and we gave quarter to those who desired it. Leaders yielded to us and we granted riches to each one who so desired. Then I lost Sigurd. It was a small matter to be called a widow, but what distresses me most is that I came to you, whereas before I was married to the most noble of kings. You have never left a battle without being bested."

King Atli replied: "That is not true, but such discussions will better neither your lot nor mine, for I have been defeated. Now behave properly toward me and have my body prepared with splendor." She said: "That I will do. I will have a magnificent burial prepared and a fine stone sarcophagus built for you. I will have you wrapped in fair cloths and consider your every need." After this Atli died and Gudrun did as she had promised. Then she had the hall set afire. When the king's retainers awoke in fear, they could not stand the flames. Instead they hewed at one another and thus they died. There ended the lives of King Atli and all his retainers.

Gudrun did not want to live after these deeds, but her final day had not yet come. People say the Volsungs and the Gjukungs were the mightiest and the most fearlessly resolute of men, as it is told in all the ancient lays. Thus the conflict was brought to an end with these events.

## 41    CONCERNING GUDRUN

Gudrun and Sigurd had a daughter called Svanhild. She was the fairest of all women and had keen eyes like her father's, so that few dared to face her glance. She transcended other women in her beauty as the sun does the other heavenly bodies.

Once Gudrun went to the sea, picked up stones in her arms, and walked out into the water, meaning to kill herself. Then towering waves carried her out over the sea. Crossing the water with their help, she came at last to the fortress of King Jonakr, a powerful ruler with many followers. He married Gudrun. Their children were Hamdir, Sorli, and Erp. Svanhild was raised there.

## 42    SVANHILD IS MARRIED AND TRAMPLED TO DEATH UNDER THE HOOVES OF HORSES

There was in those times a powerful king called Jormunrek. His son was named Randver. The king called his son to speak with him and said: "You will travel with my counselor Bikki on a mission for me to King Jonakr. Svanhild, the daughter of Sigurd Fafnir's Bane, has been raised there, and I know her to be the fairest maiden under the sun. More than any other woman I would like to marry her, and you are to ask for her hand in my name." Randver replied: "I am obliged, sir, to travel on your errand." Then he had the journey prepared in a fitting manner. They traveled until they came to King Jonakr. They saw Svanhild and thought her beauty most worthy. Randver met with the king and said: "King Jormunrek wants to offer you his kinship by marriage. He has heard of Svanhild and wants to choose her as his wife. She could hardly be given to a man who is more powerful." King Jonakr called it a splendid match and said: "Jormunrek is a king of great renown."

Gudrun said: "Fortune is too fragile a thing to trust that it not break." But with the exhortations of the king and all things considered, an agreement was reached. Svanhild went to the ship with a splendid following and sat on the raised deck next to the king's son. Then Bikki spoke to Randver: "It would be more proper for you to have so beautiful a wife, rather than for an old man to have

her." That idea suited Randver's thinking well, and he spoke agree-
ably to her, as she did to him. They arrived home in their own
land and met with the king. Bikki said: "It behooves you, my lord,
to know what has happened, although it is difficult to relate. Yet
it has to do with deceits against you. Your son has received Svanhild's full love, and she is his mistress. Do not let such a wrong go
unpunished."

In the past Bikki had given the king much bad counsel, although this outstripped any of his previous ill advice. The king listened to his many wicked persuasions. He could not still his anger
and ordered that Randver should be taken and hanged on the gallows. When Randver was led to the gallows, he took a hawk,
plucked from it all its feathers, and said that it should be shown
to his father. When the king saw it, he said: "One can see that he
thinks I am shorn of honor just as this hawk is shorn of feathers."
Jormunrek then ordered Randver removed from the gallows, but
Bikki had been busy in the meantime and Randver was dead.

Bikki spoke again: "No one deserves worse from you than
Svanhild. Let her die in disgrace." The king answered: "I accept
your advice." Then Svanhild was bound in the gate of the fortress
and horses were driven at her. But when she opened her eyes the
horses did not dare trample on her. When Bikki saw this, he commanded that a skin bag be drawn over her head. Thus it was done,
and then she died.

## 43 GUDRUN URGES HER SONS TO AVENGE SVANHILD

Gudrun heard of Svanhild's violent death and she spoke to her
sons: "How can you sit there so peacefully or speak with cheerful
words, when Jormunrek has had your sister shamefully trampled
to death under the hooves of horses? You do not have the spirit of
Gunnar or of Hogni. They would avenge their kinswoman." Hamdir answered: "Little did you praise Gunnar and Hogni when they
killed Sigurd and you were reddened with his blood. Vile was the
vengeance for your brothers when you killed your sons by Atli. We
might better kill King Jormunrek if we were all together. But we
cannot endure your taunts; so persistently are we being urged."

Gudrun went laughing and gave them drink from deep goblets. Afterward she chose large sturdy coats of mail and other armor for them. Then Hamdir said: "Here we shall part for the last time. You will hear the tidings and will hold a funeral feast for us and Svanhild." Then they departed.

Gudrun went to her chamber, her sorrow yet heavier, and said: "I have been married to three men. First I wedded Sigurd the slayer of Fafnir and he was betrayed, bringing me my deepest sorrow. Then I was given to King Atli, yet my heart was so full of hatred against him that in my grief I killed our sons. Then I went into the sea, but I was borne to land by waves, and I was married to this king. Then I married off Svanhild, sending her away to a foreign land with enormous wealth; when she was trampled under the feet of horses it was the most grievous of my sorrows after Sigurd. It was grimmest for me when Gunnar was placed in the snake pit, but it was harshest when the heart was cut out of Hogni. Better if Sigurd would come to meet me and I would go with him. Not a son, not a daughter is left here to comfort me. Do you remember now, Sigurd, what we spoke of, when we entered one bed? You said you would visit me from Hel and then wait there for me." [108] Thus ended her lamentations.

## 44    CONCERNING THE SONS OF GUDRUN. THE FINAL CHAPTER.

It is now to be told of Gudrun's sons that she had prepared their armor so that iron could not bite through it. She cautioned her sons to cause no one damage with stones[109] or other large objects, telling them they would come to harm if they did not do as she said. After they had set out they met their brother Erp and asked how he would help them. He answered: "As the hand helps the hand, or the foot helps the foot." They took this reply to mean that he would not help them at all, and so they killed him.[110]

Gudrun's sons continued on their way, and it was but a short time before Hamdir stumbled and threw out his hand. "Erp must have told the truth," he said. "I would have fallen just then, if I had not braced myself with my hand." A short time later Sorli stumbled. He threw out his foot, regained his balance, and said: "I would have fallen just then if I had not supported myself with both feet." Thus they decided that they had wronged their brother Erp.

They journeyed until they came to King Jormunrek's. They went before him and attacked at once. Hamdir cut off both his hands and Sorli both his feet. Then Hamdir said: "His head would now be off if our brother Erp were alive, whom we killed on the way. Too late we have realized this." As the verse relates:

30. Off would now be the head
    If Erp were living,
    Our battle-eager brother
    Whom we killed on the way.

In the action the brothers had not observed their mother's wishes, as they had used stones to wound. Now men attacked them, but they defended themselves bravely and well, killing many of the attackers. Iron was of no avail against the brothers. Then a one-eyed man, tall and ancient, came up and said: "You are not wise if you do not know how to kill these men." King Jormunrek answered: "Advise us how, if you can." He said: "You should stone them to death." Thus it was done and from all directions stones flew at them. So ended the lives of Hamdir and Sorli.

# Notes

1. Oðin, foremost among Norse deities, was the god of war, wisdom, ecstasy, and poetry. Known as the All-father, he was regarded as an ancestor of many Scandinavian, Anglo-Saxon, and other Germanic royal houses. The element *sig* (victory), which appears in proper names in the Volsung family, may emphasize the special relationship that existed between the Volsungs and Odin, who was also called *Sigtýr*, victory god.

2. In this sentence and in the one that follows, the manuscript is partly illegible. The full translation is taken from a later paper copy of the original manuscript.

3. *Breðafönn*, "Bredi's drift," literally means snowdrift or glacier. The proper name Bredi is derived from *breðafönn*; the reverse derivation described in the saga is a folk etymology. The name *Skaði*, derived from the word for ski or snowshoe, occurs elsewhere in Old Icelandic literature as the name of a goddess (originally a giantess) who goes about in the winter hunting with bow and arrow. It has been suggested that the episode of Skadi, Sigi, and Bredi is based on an otherwise lost myth.

4. The text says both killed and murdered (*myrðan*), reflecting the Norse distinction between manslaughter and murder. After the act, if the killer publicly announced his deed, it was manslaughter, an offense that could be atoned for with wergild. If, however, there

was no announcement, or if the killing was performed in stealth, it was murder. The killer was then referred to as a *morð-vargr*, murderer (literally, killer wolf), and was beyond the pale of the law.

5. *Vargr* (wolf or monster) was used in Icelandic law codes to refer to outlaws (see n. 4), who could be hunted down like wolves. The phrase "wolf in hallowed places" suggests an outlaw guilty of murder or of a particularly serious offense, especially committing a crime within a hallowed place or sanctuary.

6. *Ríkr* traditionally means powerful or mighty in Old Norse. A new sense of the word, that of being rich or wealthy, appeared near the end of the thirteenth century and was probably influenced by foreign usage. Since this manuscript was written down sometime between 1200 and 1270, I have chosen to employ the traditional meaning.

7. The Huns were regarded in Germanic heroic legend as just another Germanic people. In the *Prose Edda* Snorri Sturluson places Sigi's kingdom in Frakkland, or France.

8. These lines are somewhat convoluted. The sense of the passage is that Rerir is caught between a rock and a hard place: he must either kill his maternal uncles or let his father go unavenged.

9. The wife of Odin. In "Oddrun's Lament" both Frigg and the goddess Freya are invoked for aid in childbirth.

10. *Óskmær* (wish-maiden) is a rare term. It may come from *óskamær,* chosen or adopted maiden, i.e., stepdaughter. Here it refers to a woman who may be a valkyrie, one of the supernatural women associated with Odin. The valkyries were Odin's chosen maids. Valkyries haunted battlefields, granting victory and choosing those who were to die. The literal meaning of *valkyrja* is "chooser of the slain."

11. The ability to put on a shape made of feathers, i.e., a bird shape, is commonly attributed to supernatural women in Old Icelandic literature.

12. *Haugr,* mound or how, is a term often found in Old Icelandic writings. On occasion a mound close to the house of an estate is mentioned, and from such a vantage point a master would survey his property. *Haugr* also means cairn or burial mound and in some instances refers to a kind of sacrificial mound. It is not clear which meaning is intended here.

13. The passage does not state clearly who ate the apple. Although it might seem logical for the queen to consume the fruit, the grammar favors the king. My thanks to Stefán Karlsson of the Stofnun Árnamagnússonar for his advice on this passage.

14. Warriors killed in battle were believed to go to Valhalla (Hall of the Slain) to join Odin, for whom they would fight in the final battle that will result in the destruction of the world. A man dying in bed might be marked with the point of a spear, a weapon sacred to Odin, so that he could go to Valhalla.

15. For the meaning of the name Volsung, see Introduction.

16. *Eik* means oak but the Icelanders often used the word as a general term for tree.

17. *Barnstokkr* literally means child-trunk (Bairnstock), although it is not clear that this was its original meaning. In this passage the tree is called *eik* (oak) (see n. 16). A few passages farther on it is called *apaldr* (apple tree), another general term for tree. *Apaldr,* however, may have a further symbolic meaning, possibly being associated with the apple tree of the goddess Idunn. *Barnstokkr* may also be identified with the world tree Yggdrasil. It is also conceivable that the word was originally *bran(d)stokkr,* the first part of the compound being derived from *brandr,* brand or firebrand, a word sometimes synonymous with "hearth." If so, the word may originally have been connected with the fire burning in the hall.

18. Odin is often portrayed in the legendary sagas as visiting men in such a disguise. His headgear, referred to as a deep hood, was probably a form of hat. The story of how Odin lost his eye to obtain wisdom is told by Snorri in the *Prose Edda.*

19. *Kynfylgja* literally means family fetch. A fetch was a guardian spirit or a supernatural attendant, usually female, associated with an individual or a family. The term is used here with the more abstract meaning of inherited characteristic or (bad) luck.

20. *Jarðhús* literally means earth house, apparently some form of a dugout.

21. The generic term "man" is used and may mean an assistant, a companion, or here a boy with manly qualities.

22. It was customary to fasten together the ends of sleeves by stitching them just above the hands.

23. In this sentence and in the preceding one, the manuscript is partly illegible. The full translation is taken from a later paper copy of the original manuscript.

24. It appears that the leaf is sent by Odin. In Norse mythology, ravens are associated with Odin. Snorri calls Odin *Hrafnaguð* (God of Ravens), and the raven is called Odin's swan or Odin's seagull. Odin had two ravens called Hugin and Munin (Thought and Memory) who flew off every day. When they returned, they perched on the god's shoulders and told him of events throughout the world.

25. Norns were supernatural women who controlled the fates of men. In the *Prose Edda,* Snorri says that there are three Norns: Urd, Verdandi, and Skuld (Past, Present, and Future). Other sources, however, say that there are Norns belonging to the races of gods, elves, and dwarfs, and beyond Snorri's three great ones there were many others. These supernatural women are often associated with specific individuals; for example, a Norn would be present at an individual's birth to determine his fate. The use of the indefinite form here in the text makes it likely that the latter type of Norn is meant.

26. *Laukr* (leek) may also refer to garlic. Both leek and garlic are considered in many cultures to have magical or medicinal properties.

27. Hringstead has been identified as Ringsted on the island of Zealand. Ringsted was at times a royal Danish residence. Like most other place-names in this part of the saga, however, Hringstead is almost impossible to identify with certainty. Solfell (*Solfjöll*) literally means mountains of the sun.

28. There were many kings, some of whom did not rule over a country but controlled an army. Independent military leaders who commanded ships were often called sea kings.

29. Norvasund usually denotes the Strait of Gibraltar, but not in this instance. In the equivalent passage in "The First Lay of Helgi Hunding's Bane," the name is written Orvasund.

30. The conversation that follows is a *senna,* or contest of insults. Such contests are frequent in Old Icelandic literature. Most of the insults in this *senna* make use of one of the worst possible affronts in the culture, i.e., accusations of effeminacy or passive homosexuality. In Iceland, to accuse someone of passive homosexuality was an offense punishable by outlawry.

31. In the preceding passage Granmar is Hodbrodd's father, not his brother. In "The Second Lay of Helgi Hunding's Bane," this *senna* takes place between Sinfjotli and Gudmund.

32. *Minni* (ancient lore) also means the memorial cup or toast at feasts and sacrifices.

33. Asgard was the realm of the gods, as opposed to *Miðgarð* (Middle-Earth), the abode of men.

34. Later in the saga, Grani is the name of Sigurd's horse.

35. *Fyrir Grindum* (in front of Grindir) may mean ships anchored at dock.

36. These women may be valkyries.

37. Odin again. One of Odin's functions was that of psychopomp, guide to the world of the dead.

38. I.e., allowed to purchase provisions.

39. The meaning of the passage may be that Sigmund took over the running of Eylimi's kingdom, but the text is vague.

40. *Spádísir* (spaewomen) literally means prophetic female spirits. The *dísir* were guardian spirits who played a minor cultic role. *Spádísir* is often used in a generalized or metaphorical sense to refer to valkyries, Norns, or goddesses. Here it would seem to be Norns, deciding men's fate.

41. Odin once again.

42. *Ótta,* the last part of the night just before daybreak.

43. Fosterage was a Norse custom of having a child raised in another household in order to extend kinship bonds or to form political alliances.

44. Runes are the characters of the alphabet used by the Germanic peoples for writing on wood or stone. They had both magical and practical uses.

45. Odin's eight-legged horse.

46. The passage may also be read, "I know of the kin of this serpent."

47. Loki is the trickster in Old Norse myth. He is an ambiguous figure, sometimes on the side of the giants, sometimes on the side of the gods. The two aspects of his character are evident in this tale: he places the gods in danger, only to rescue them himself.

48. Hœnir is a relatively obscure god who figures in several myths dealing with the origin of the gods and men.

49. The Æsir are the chief gods of Old Norse myth.

50. Goddess of the sea.

51. Hel, the daughter of Loki and a giantess, is the goddess of the underworld. The name is sometimes used to denote the underworld itself, as in "travel the road to Hel," but it is not to be confused with the Christian Hell.

52. A kenning for gold.

53. Here Odin is almost certainly a mistake. In the same stanza from "The Lay of Regin," Andvari says his father is called Oin. Oin is also a dwarf name from the Eddic poem "Völuspá" ("Sibyl's Prophecy").

54. The ring acquired from the dwarf Andvari, above. *Andvaranautr* literally means Andvari's gift.

55. Several of the later manuscripts begin chapter 15 here, a more logical point in the narrative.

56. Hugin may refer to one of Odin's two ravens. More probably the word refers not to any specific raven but to a *huginn*, a poetic synonym for raven. "To gladden the raven" meant "to kill men in battle."

57. Fjolnir is, again, Odin.

58. Odin once again.

59. According to the "Lay of Fafnir," Sigurd withheld his name because of an ancient belief that a dying man could curse his enemy if he knew the enemy's name.

60. *Ægishjálmr,* "helm of terror," refers to an object (helmet?), probably magical and certainly precious, which Sigurd later takes from Fafnir's lair.

61. A dwarf.

62. A reference to Ragnarok, the end of the world. Surt is a fire-giant who, after defeating the god Frey at the final battle, will cover the world with flame.

63. The land of the Franks, France.

64. A kenning for warrior.

65. *Gamanræðna* here, but in the Eddic "Lay of Sigrdrifa" *gamanrúna* is found. The meaning then would be runes of joy or pleasure.

66. The rune with the phonetic value [t] was named after the god Tyr.

67. Ships.

68. Assembly.

69. Odin.

70. Arvak and Alsvid are the horses that draw the chariot of the sun across the sky.

71. Spelled Rognir in the manuscript but almost certainly the giant (H)rungnir.

72. Bragi, a god of poetry. Bragi may have been a ninth-century Norwegian poet who was elevated to the status of god by later writers.

73. Probably a reference to Bifrost, the bridge of the gods.

74. Gaupnir is spelled Gungnir in "The Lay of Sigrdrifa." Gungnir was Odin's spear.

75. The mead of poetry, the story of which is explained in Snorri's *Prose Edda*.

76. The Vanir are a family of gods particularly associated with fertility.

77. The manuscript says *bókrúnar* (beech runes) but probably should be *bótrúnar* (cure runes).

78. A reference to Ragnarok.

79. A kenning for warrior.

80. *Væringjar,* Vaerings or Varangians, were Scandinavian traders in Russia. The name also denotes Northmen serving in the bodyguard of the Byzantine emperor. Here the term may simply denote "Scandinavians."

81. *Kurteisi* (courtesy), a borrowing from Old French romance, was translated into Old Norse in the thirteenth century. The concept itself is foreign to Scandinavia.

82. *Hild* (battle) is a common element in women's names in Old Norse. The element *bekk* literally means bench.

83. *Bryn,* from *brynja,* means mail coat.

84. At this point the saga begins the move from myth into legend. For the history underlying the saga, see Introduction.

85. Attila the Hun.

86. Apparently the brother of Helgi. The name Hamund, missing in the saga manuscript, is found in an account in Saxo Grammaticus's history.

87. Two and a half years. The Norse year was divided into two seasons.

88. Russia.

89. Aslaug links *The Saga of the Volsungs* and *The Saga of Ragnar Lodbrok.*

90. Gunnar, it seems.

91. Probably an allusion to Brynhild's being a valkyrie.

92. *Til borða* is ambiguous and the line may also mean: "We will go to the table to eat and. . . ."

93. Presumably the reference is to Grimhild's "ale of forgetfulness," which Sigurd consumed in chapter 28.

94. A kenning for serpent.

95. *Geri*, the "ravener," Odin's wolf.

96. Atli's sister.

97. *Leiðsla* means a burial, but it also has the metaphoric sense of being led through a vision of the afterlife.

98. According to widespread medieval belief, the arteries were considered to be ducts of air, whereas the veins were understood to be passages for blood.

99. *Skógr* (forest or woods) is the outlaws' home, the wilderness.

100. This enigmatic passage is based on "Guðrúnarkviða hin forna," stanza 21.

101. Ling-fish is a kenning for serpent.

102. The Haddings were legendary Viking princes, and the Haddings' land is the sea. The "ling-fish of the Haddings' land" is most likely an eel or a sea snake. Another interpretation might be a ship.

103. The uncut corn of the Haddings' land would be kelp or seaweed.

104. The meaning of the line is unclear. *Innleið* may mean inroad.

105. Here these female spirits play a role similar to that of the fetch. Their appearance forebodes death.

106. Kostbera.

107. *Niflungr* literally means son of mist. In the *Nibelungenlied,* the Nibelungs (Niflungs) possess the treasure that Sigfried wins. Af-

ter the Burgundians obtain the gold, they inherit the name "Nibelungs" as well.

108. A difficult passage. Literally it reads: "You said you would visit me and wait for me from Hel."

109. This and the following passage concerning the use of stones may also be translated with the sense that the sons are not to harm stones. If one adopts the second translation, it is possible that the line has something to do with an interdiction against allowing blood to pollute stones or the stony earth. It may be that an incident in which the brothers inflict damage on stones has been dropped from this rendering of the story. However this may be, by the end of the episode stones were able (and willing?) to do what iron could not.

110. In the *Prose Edda* Snorri Sturluson tells us that the brothers killed Erp because he enjoyed his mother's affection, and they were angered by her taunting. The Eddic poem "Hamðismál," however, calls Erp the son of a different mother.

# EDDIC POEMS USED BY THE SAGA AUTHOR

In writing his prose work the saga writer probably had at his disposal an earlier, now lost, manuscript of Eddic lays. It is also probable that the sagaman knew oral variants of the poems. In either event, the verses employed by the writer differ at times from the extant poems contained in the *Codex Regius*.

Atlakviða (The Lay of Atli)

Atlamál in grœnlenzku (The Greenlandic Lay of Atli)

Brot af Sigurðarkviðu (Fragment of a Sigurd Lay)

Fáfnismál (The Lay of Fafnir)

Guðrúnarkviða in forna (The Old Lay of Gudrun)

Guðrúnarhvöt (Gudrun's Enciting)

Grípisspá (The Prophecy of Gripir)

Helgakviða Hundingsbana I (The First Lay of Helgi Hunding's Bane)

Hamðismál (The Lay of Hamdir)

Reginsmál (The Lay of Regin)

Sigrdrífumál (The Lay of Sigrdrifa)

Sigurðarkviða in skamma (The Short Lay of Sigurd)

The saga author also used a prose section of the Edda:
Frá dauða Sinfjötla (About the Death of Sinfjotli)

# GLOSSARY

This glossary lists names of persons (human or supernatural), groups, places, animals, and objects that appear in the saga. Entries are alphabetized in anglicized form, followed by the normalized Old Icelandic within parentheses. The numbers refer to chapters, and brackets signify that a character plays an important part in the chapter without being explicitly named there.

Æsir (*Æsir*), the Norse gods: **14**, kill Otr, are forced to pay Andvari's gold in compensation for him; **18**, some of the Norns belong to the race of the Æsir; the Æsir and Surt will mix together their blood on the island called Oskapt; **21**, received the runes.

Agnar or Audabrodir (*Agnarr* or *Auðabróðir*): **21**, a king who fought Hjalmgunnar. Odin had promised victory to Hjalmgunnar, but Brynhild granted victory to Agnar.

Alf (*Álfr Hjálpreksson*): **12**, son of King Hjalprek of Denmark; plans to marry Hjordis; **13**, marries Hjordis; is Sigurd's guardian; [**17**, equips Sigurd for expedition to avenge Sigmund]; **26**, allusion to the marriage of Sigurd's mother to Alf.

Alf (*Álfr Hundingsson*): **9**, son of Hunding; killed by Helgi.

Alf the Old (*Álfr inn gamli*): **9**, fights with Granmar and Hodbrodd against Helgi and Sinfjotli.

Alsvid (*Alsviðr*), one of the horses that draw the chariot of the sun across the sky: **21**, runes were cut on Alsvid's head.

Alsvid (*Alsviðr Heimisson*): **24**, son of Heimir; **25**, tries to dissuade Sigurd from courtship of Brynhild.

Andvaranaut (*Andvaranautr*): **14**, a ring from Andvari's hoard, seized by Loki; Andvari puts a curse on it, that it will be the death of whoever owns it; Odin attempts to keep it for himself, but is forced to give it to Hreidmar; [although not explicitly mentioned, Andvaranaut forms part of Fafnir's hoard, which Sigurd wins]; **29**, Sigurd takes from Brynhild the ring Andvaranaut, which he had given to her earlier (presumably, in chap. 25); **30**, Gudrun shows Brynhild Andvaranaut and reveals that it was Sigurd, not Gunnar, who had taken it from her.

Andvari (*Andvari*): **14**, a dwarf who lives in a waterfall in the shape of a pike; Loki catches the pike and forces him to give up his gold treasure in ransom for his life; he puts a curse on the ring Andvaranaut, that it will be the death of whoever owns it.

Andvari's Fall (*Andvarafors*): **14**, waterfall where Otr fishes in the shape of an otter and Andvari lives in the shape of a pike.

Arvak (*Árvakr*), one of the horses that draw the chariot of the sun across the sky: **21**, runes were cut on Arvak's ear.

Asgard (*Ásgarðr*), the home of the gods: **9**, insult directed at Granmar, "You were a valkyrie in Asgard."

Aslaug (*Áslaugr*): **29**, daughter of Sigurd and Brynhild (presumably begotten in chap. 25).

Atli (*Atli Buðlason*), Attila the Hun: **26**, brother of Brynhild; **27**, Brynhild predicts that Gudrun will marry and then kill King Atli; **29**, Budli's son; present at feast at Brynhild's marriage to Gunnar; **32**, Gunnar taunts Brynhild that she deserves to see King Atli killed; upon dying, Brynhild prophesies Gunnar's death at Atli's hands and Atli's death at Gudrun's hands; **34**, Gudrun is married, against her will, to Atli; **35**, has dreams prophesying his sons' deaths; desires the gold that was Sigurd's; treacherously invites Gunnar and Hogni to his house with the intention of getting it; **36**, Hogni's wife has prophetic dreams of Atli's treachery; **38**, Atli attacks Gunnar and Hogni when they arrive at his hall; **39**, Atli captures Gunnar and Hogni, cuts out Hogni's heart, and puts Gunnar in a snake pit to die; **40**, Gudrun kills her sons by Atli and gives him their blood and hearts to eat; then she kills Atli; **43**, Gudrun laments her disastrous marriage to Atli.

Audabrodir (*Auðabróðir*). *See* Agnar.

Barnstock (*Barnstokkr*): **2**, tree in Volsung's hall; **3**, [Odin] thrusts sword into Barnstock.

Bekkhild (*Bekkhildr Buðladóttir*): **24**, daughter of Budli, wife of Heimir, sister of Brynhild.

Bera. *See* Kostbera.

Bikki (*Bikki*), counselor of King Jormunrek: **32**, upon dying, Brynhild prophesies Svanhild's downfall through the counsels of Bikki; **42**, slanderously accuses Randver and Svanhild of being lovers and contrives their deaths.

Borghild (*Borghildr*): **8**, marries Sigmund; mother of Helgi and Hamund; **10**, poisons her stepson Sinfjotli.

Bragi (*Bragi*), god of poetry: **21**, runes were cut on Bragi's tongue.

Bravoll (*Brávöllr*), a battlefield: **9**, Sinfjotli's insult to Granmar, "You were a mare . . . and I rode you . . . on Bravoll."

Bredi (*Breði*): **1**, thrall of Skadi, killed by Sigi.

Bredi's Drift (*Breðafönn*): **1**, snowdrift, so called because Sigi buried the murdered Bredi in the drift.

Brynhild (*Brynhildr Buðladóttir*), daughter of Budli: **20**, birds advise Sigurd to ride to Hindarfell, where Brynhild sleeps; **21**, Sigurd awakens her from the sleep that Odin has placed upon her; she teaches him runes; **22**, gives Sigurd wise advice; he pledges to marry her; **24**, sister of Bekkhild; is so named because she takes up a mail coat and goes into battle; **25**, foster daughter of Heimir; daughter of Budli; a shield-maiden; weaves Sigurd's deeds into a tapestry; accepts Sigurd's courtship but predicts that he will marry Gudrun instead of her; **26**, Gudrun visits her and they discuss famous men; Brynhild praises Sigurd; **27**, interprets Gudrun's dream; **28**, Sigurd forgets Brynhild when Grimhild gives him a magic drink; Gunnar decides to win Brynhild; **29**, Sigurd in the shape of Gunnar rides through her wall of flame; she marries Gunnar; **30**, she and Gudrun quarrel, and Gudrun reveals that it was Sigurd who rode through the wall of flame; **31**, sulks in her bed; refuses Gunnar's attempts to reconcile her; in dialogue with Sigurd, pours out her love and hatred for him; says that someone must die, for she will not have two husbands in one hall; **32**, urges Gunnar to kill Sigurd; laments Sigurd's death and stabs herself; prophesies the future of the Gjukungs; **33**, asks to be burned on Sigurd's pyre; dies.

Budli (*Buðli*): **25**, father of Brynhild; **26**, a king; **29**, gives his consent to Brynhild's marriage to Gunnar; father of Atli; **31**, Brynhild claims that Budli forced her to marry against her will; the sons of Gjuki killed Budli's unnamed brother; **40**, Atli accuses Gudrun of being greedy for King Budli's lands.

Busiltjorn (*Busiltjörn*): **13**, a river; Sigurd chooses a horse by driving a herd of horses into the river and taking the only one that does not swim back to shore.

Denmark (*Danmörk*): **12**, kingdom of Hjalprek and Alf; **34**, Gudrun takes refuge in Denmark with King Half; Valdemar of Denmark is mentioned.

Disir (*Dísir*), minor, often guardian goddesses: **11**, Sigmund's spaewomen (*spádísir*) watched over him; **21**, invoke the *disir* for aid in childbirth; **37**, Glaumvor's premonitory dream of Gunnar's death; somber-looking women chose Gunnar as husband; Glaum-vor interprets them as Gunnar's disir.

Dvalin (*Dvalinn*), a dwarf: **18**, some of the Norns are daughters of Dvalin.

Elves (*Alfar*), a race of supernatural beings: **18**, some of the Norns belong to the race of elves; **21**, received the runes.

Erp (*Erpr Jónakrsson*): **41**, Gudrun's son by Jonak; **44**, Hamdir and Sorli kill Erp, then regret it because their revenge against Jormunrek would have succeeded if Erp had been alive to cut off Jormunrek's head.

Eyjolf (*Eyjólfr Hundingsson*): **9**, killed by Helgi.

Eylimi (*Eylimi*): **11**, a king, father of Hjordis; **12**, falls in battle against Lyngvi; **26**, Sigurd praised for avenging Eylimi.

Eymod (*Eymóðr*): **34**, accompanies the sons of Gjuki on their journey to Denmark to be reconciled with Gudrun.

Fafnir (*Fáfnir*): **13**, Regin tells Sigurd that Fafnir, as a serpent, lies on great wealth; **14**, kills his father Hreidmar; turns into an evil serpent [dragon] and lies on the hoard of gold; **15**, the sword is made with which Fafnir can be slain; **16**, **17**, Regin urges Sigurd to slay him; **18**, is slain by Sigurd; **19**, Regin drinks his blood; Sigurd roasts his heart, tastes his blood, and understands the speech of birds; **20**, Sigurd takes Fafnir's hoard; **21**, Sigurd identified as the one who has the helmet of Fafnir and carries Fafnir's bane in his hand; **23**, Sigurd slew the dragon called Fafnir by the Vaerings; **28**, Sigurd gives Gudrun some of Fafnir's heart to eat; she becomes grimmer and wiser than before; **29**, Sigurd in the guise of Gunnar gives Brynhild a ring from Fafnir's hoard; **30**, Sigurd's slaying of Fafnir is cited by both Gudrun and Brynhild as a mark of his superiority over Gunnar; **31**, Brynhild had declared herself betrothed to the one who had Fafnir's inheritance; **33**, **42**, **43**, Sigurd described as the bane of Fafnir.

Feng (*Fengr*): **17**, a byname of Odin.

Fjolnir (*Fjölnir*): **17**, a byname of Odin.

Fjon (*Fjón*), Danish island: **34**, Gudrun and Thora's tapestry shows the battle of Sigar and Siggeir in the south of Fjon.

Fjornir (*Fjórnir*), Gunnar's cupbearer: **37**, Gunnar asks him for wine, for it may be Gunnar's last entertainment.

Frakkland (*Frakkland*), the land of the Franks: **21**, Sigurd is going toward Frakkland when he comes upon the sleeping Brynhild.

Franks (*Frakkar*), a Germanic people: **34**, accompany the sons of Gjuki on their journey to Denmark to be reconciled with Gudrun.

Frekastein (*Frekasteinn*): **9**, the place where Helgi and Sinfjotli do battle against Granmar and Hodbrodd.

Frigg (*Frigg*), a goddess, the wife of Odin: **1**, conveys to Odin Rerir's prayers for a child.

Gardakonungr (*Garðakonungr*): **29**, Brynhild says she went to battle with this king.

Gaupnir (*Gaupnir*), perhaps a manuscript mistake for Gungnir, Odin's sword: **21**, runes were cut on the point of Gaupnir.

Gautland (*Gautland*), region that is today in Sweden: **3**, **4**, **5**, Siggeir's kingdom.

Gjuki (*Gjúki*): **25**, father of Gudrun; **26**, king of a kingdom south of the Rhine; father of Gunnar, Hogni, Guttorm, and Gudrun; married to Grimhild; **27**, mentioned; **28**, Sigurd visits him, receives his daughter in marriage, and swears brotherhood with his sons; **29**, mentioned as father of Gunnar; **31**, several allusions to the sons of Gjuki.

Gjukungs (*Gjúkungar*), descendants of Gjuki: **26**, **39**, fight with Atli; **40**, mentioned.

Glaumvor (*Glaumvör*): **35**, Gunnar's wife; **37**, has prophetic dreams of Atli's treachery.

Gnipalund (*Gnipalundr*): **9**, harbor to which Sigrun directs Helgi.

Gnitaheath (*Gnitaheiðr*): **13**, the place where Fafnir, as a serpent, lies upon great wealth; **35**, Gunnar and Hogni have all the gold that lay on Gnitaheath.

Golnir (*Gölnir*), a giant: **9**, insult directed at Granmar, "You were the goatherd of the giant Golnir."

Goti (*Goti*) Gunnar's horse: **29**, refuses to pass through Brynhild's wall of flame.

Gram (*Gramr*): **12**, the fragments of Sigmund's broken sword will be mended and made into a sword named Gram; **15**, Regin forges Gram; **17**, Sigurd does battle against Lyngvi with the sword Gram; **19**, Sigurd cleans the sword Gram after slaying Fafnir with it; **20**, Sigurd beheads Regin with Gram; **23**, seven spans long; **29**, when Sigurd in Gunnar's shape rides through Brynhild's wall of flame, he sleeps with Brynhild in one bed with Gram unsheathed between them.

Grani (*Grani*), Sigurd's horse: **9**, insult directed at Granmar, "You were a mare with the stallion Grani"; **13**, chosen by Sigurd with Odin's advice; **20**, Sigurd loads Fafnir's treasure on Grani's back; **25**, mopes when Sigurd is lovesick for Brynhild; **28**, Sigurd rides Grani to Gjuki's hall; **29**, refuses to go through the wall of flame with Gunnar on his back; carries Sigurd through the flames; **30**, Gudrun excuses Gunnar's failure to ride through the fire by pointing out that Grani refused to carry him; **31**, Brynhild had declared herself betrothed to the one who would ride Grani through her wall of flame; **32**, Atli had asked if Brynhild would marry the man who rode Grani; **34**, Gudrun describes how Grani mourned Sigurd's death.

Granmar (*Granmarr*): **9**, a king, the father of Hodbrodd; engages in a *senna*, or contest of insults, with Sinfjotli; does battle with Helgi; is defeated.

GLOSSARY

Greek Ocean (*Grikklandshaf*), the Aegean Sea: **23**, Sigurd's name is known in all tongues north of the Greek Ocean.

Grimhild (*Grímhildr*): **26**, a sorceress, wife of King Gjuki; **27**, Brynhild predicts that Grimhild will give Sigurd bespelled mead; **28**; gives Sigurd drink so he forgets Brynhild; connives Sigurd's marriage to Gudrun; urges Gunnar to court Brynhild; **29**, has taught Sigurd and Gunnar how to exchange shapes; **30, 31**, Brynhild blames Grimhild for her misfortunes; **32**, incites Guttorm to kill Sigurd; **34**, urges her sons to reconcile themselves with Gudrun; gives Gudrun a magic drink of forgetfulness; urges Gudrun to marry Atli.

Gripir (*Grípir*): **16**, Sigurd's mother's brother; prophesies Sigurd's fate.

Gudrun (*Guðrún Gjúkadóttir*): **25**, Brynhild predicts that Sigurd will marry Gudrun; **26**, daughter of King Gjuki; visits Brynhild to tell her dreams; **27**, Brynhild interprets Gudrun's dreams; **28**, is married to Sigurd; **30**, she and Brynhild quarrel; **31**, sends others to placate Brynhild; **32**, awakes to find Sigurd fatally wounded in her arms; upon dying, Brynhild prophesies Gudrun's future misfortunes; **34**, Gudrun laments Sigurd; takes refuge with King Half of Denmark; is reconciled with her brothers and given a magic drink of forgetfulness by Grimhild; is married to Atli, although she foresees misfortune from it; **35**, sends her brothers a ring wound with wolf's hair bearing a runic message to warn of Atli's treachery; **38**, dons mail coat and fights beside her brothers against Atli; **39**, Gudrun sends Gunnar a harp in the snake pit; **40**, Gudrun kills her sons by Atli and gives him their blood and hearts to eat; then she kills Atli and burns his hall; **41**, has daughter Svanhild by Sigurd; tries to drown herself, but is carried by the waves across the sea; marries King Jonakr, by whom she has sons Hamdir, Sorli, and Erp; **42**, has doubts about Svanhild's marriage to Jormunrek; **43**, incites her sons to avenge Svanhild; laments her sorrows; **44**, provides her sons with armor that iron will not bite; warns them not to harm stones.

Gunnar (*Gunnarr Gjúkason*): **26**, son of King Gjuki; **28**, offers his sister Gudrun to Sigurd in marriage; swears brotherhood with Sigurd; decides to win Brynhild as his wife; **29**, fails to ride through Brynhild's wall of flame; changes shapes with Sigurd, who performs the feat; Brynhild marries him, believing that he has ridden through her wall of flame; **30**, Brynhild and Gudrun quarrel over the relative merits of Gunnar and Sigurd; **31**, tries to placate Brynhild, and she pours out her contempt for him and her preference for Sigurd; **32**, incites Guttorm to kill Sigurd; upon dying, Brynhild predicts his death at Atli's hands; **33**, Brynhild asks Gunnar to burn her on Sigurd's pyre; **34**, reconciled with his sister Gudrun; **35**, accepts Atli's treacherous invitation to visit him; **37**, travels to Atli's, despite premonitions of disaster; **38**, refuses to give treasure to Atli; does battle against him; **39**, Atli captures Gunnar; when the location of the treasure is demanded of him, Gunnar asks to see Hogni's bloody heart first (so that he will know that he is the last person alive who knows the secret); Atli puts Gunnar in a snake pit, and he dies; **43**, Gudrun taunts her sons that they lack the spirit of Gunnar; she laments Gunnar's death.

Guttorm (*Guttormr Gjúkason*): **26**, son of King Gjuki; **32**, is incited to kill Sigurd; is slain by dying Sigurd; **33**, Guttorm's body is burned on the pyre with Sigurd and Brynhild.

Haddings (*Haddingjar*), legendary viking princes: **34**, "Haddings' land" is a kenning for the sea.

Hagbard (*Hagbarðr Hámundarson*), son of Hamund: **26**, Brynhild lists him as foremost of kings; Sigar took his sister and burned another sister in her house.

Hagbard (*Hagbarðr Hundingsson*), son of Hunding: **9**, killed by Helgi.

Haki (*Haki Hámundarson*): **26**, son of Hamund; Brynhild lists him as foremost of kings; Sigar took his sister and burned another sister in her house.

Hakon (*Hákon*): **34**, father of Thora, with whom Gudrun takes refuge in Denmark.

Half (*Hálfr*): **34**, after Sigurd's death Gudrun takes refuge with King Half of Denmark.

Hamdir (*Hamðir Jónakrsson*): **41**, Gudrun's son by Jonakr; **43**, Gudrun incites him and his brothers to avenge Svanhild; he responds by pointing out to Gudrun her wrongdoings; he predicts that he and his brothers will be killed; **44**, kills Erp; cuts off Jormunrek's hands; is stoned to death.

Hamund (*Hámundr*): **26**, father of Haki and Hagbard.

Hamund (*Hámundr Sigmundarson*): **8**, son of Sigmund and Borghild.

Hedinsey (*Heðinsey*), a Baltic island: **9**, place from which a company comes to join Helgi's forces.

Heimir (*Heimir*): **24**, a chieftain, married to Bekkhild, sister of Brynhild; Sigurd visits him; **25**, foster father of Brynhild; **29**, Gunnar consults him in his suit for Brynhild; Heimir directs Sigurd and Gunnar to Brynhild's wall of flame.

Hel (*Hel*), the goddess of the dead and the name of her realm: **14**, Andvari is forced to pay gold as a ransom to save his head from Hel; **18**, Sigurd sends Fafnir to Hel; **35**, Atli dreams that two hawks (symbolizing his sons) travel the road to Hel; **39**, many a man travels the road to Hel because of Gunnar's and Helgi's weapons; **43**, Gudrun recalls that Sigurd said he would wait for her in Hel.

Helgi (*Helgi Sigmundarson*): **8**, born to Sigmund and Borghild; **9**, kills Hunding and Hunding's sons; kills Hodbrodd; marries Sigrun.

Hervard (*Hervarðr Hundingsson*): **9**, son of Hunding; killed by Helgi.

Hindarfell (*Hindarfjall*), a mountain: **20**, birds advise Sigurd to ride to Hindarfell, where Brynhild sleeps; **21**, Sigurd awakens Brynhild on Hindarfell, obtains runes from her.

Hjalli (*Hjalli*): **39**, a thrall who is killed in Hogni's stead; Gunnar recognizes a heart as Hjalli's not Hogni's, because it quakes.

Hjalmgunnar (*Hjálmgunnarr*): **21**, a king who fought Agnar; Odin promised victory to Hjalmgunnar, but Brynhild struck him down in battle; in revenge, Odin stuck Brynhild with a sleep-thorn.

Hjalprek (*Hjálprekr*): **12**, king of Denmark, father of Alf; **13**, Sigurd's guardian; [**17**, equips Sigurd for expedition to avenge Sigmund]; **30**, Brynhild charges that Sigurd was a thrall of Hjalprek.

Hjordis (*Hjördís Eylimadóttir*): **11**, daughter of King Eylimi; courted by both Sigmund and Lyngvi; chooses to marry Sigmund; **12**, receives fragments of sword from dying Sigmund; is taken in a viking raid by Alf, who plans to marry her; **13**, gives birth to Sigurd; married to Alf; [**15**, gives Sigurd fragments of Sigmund's broken sword].

Hjorvard (*Hjörvarðr Hundingsson*): **17**, son of Hunding; killed by Sigurd.

Hljod (*Hljóð*), daughter of the giant Hrimnir: [**1**, Odin's wish-maiden, brings apple of fertility to Rerir]; **2**, marries Volsung.

Hlymdale (*Hlymdalir*): **29**, Heimir's home.

Hnikar (*Hnikarr*): **17**, a byname of Odin.

Hodbrodd (*Hodbroddr Granmarsson*): **9**, son of Granmar; betrothed to Sigrun, who is unwilling to marry him; killed by Helgi at Sigrun's instigation.

Hoenir (*Hœnir*), a god: **14**, is traveling with Odin and Loki when Loki kills Otr and the gods are forced to pay compensation.

Hogni (*Högni*): **9**, a king; father of Sigrun.

Hogni (*Högni Gjúkason*): **26**, son of King Gjuki; **28**, swears brotherhood with Sigurd; **29**, accompanies Gunnar and Sigurd on Gunnar's expedition to win Brynhild; **31**, fetters Brynhild when she tries to kill Gunnar; sends Sigurd to placate Brynhild; **32**, advises Gunnar against killing Sigurd; counsels Gunnar to let Brynhild die; **35**, suspects treachery in Atli's invitation, but agrees to go with Gunnar to visit Atli; **36**, dismisses his wife's prophetic dreams of Atli's treachery; **37**, goes to Atli's stronghold; breaks down the gate; beats Vingi to death; **38**, fights against Atli; hurls accusations against him; **39**, Atli captures Hogni; Gunnar demands to see Hogni's bloody heart (so he will know that the secret of the location of the treasure is safe); Hogni's heart is cut out; **40**, Hogni's son helps Gudrun kill Atli; **43**, Gudrun taunts her sons that they lack the spirit of Hogni; she laments Hogni's death.

Holkvir (*Hölkvir*): **29**, Hogni's horse.

Hreidmar (*Hreiðmarr*): **13**, father of Regin; **14**, father of Fafnir, Otr, and Regin; demands the gold of the dwarf Andvari from the gods as compensation for his slain son Otr; is killed by Fafnir.

Hrimnir (*Hrímnir*): **1**, a giant whose daughter—Odin's wish-maiden—conveys apple of fertility to Rerir; **2**, sends his daughter to Hljod to marry Volsung.

Hring's sons (*Hrings synir*): **9**, fight with Granmar and Hodbrodd against Helgi and Sinfjotli.

Hringstead (*Hringstaðir*), a place in Denmark, possibly Ringsted in Zealand: **8**, Sigmund's naming gift to Helgi.

Hropt (*Hroptr*), a name for Odin: **21**, mind runes were read, carved, and heeded by Hropt.

Hrotti (*Hrotti*): **20**, a sword that Sigurd finds in Fafnir's hoard.

Hugin (*Huginn*), Odin's raven: **17**, [Odin] says: "As Hnikar they hailed me when Hugin I gladdened."

Hunding (*Hundingr*): **9**, killed by Helgi; **11**, father of Lyngvi.

Hunding's sons (*Hundings synir*): **9**, call out an army against Helgi to avenge their father; **17**, Sigurd kills Lyngvi and Hjorvard; **26**, Sigurd praised for killing the sons of Hunding.

Hunland (*Húnaland*): **1**, ruled by Sigi; **2**, ruled by Volsung; **11**, Sigmund's kingdom; **32**, Sigurd called king of Hunland.

Huns (*Hýnir* also *Húnar*), a people of central Asia: **39**, the Rhine shall have the gold before the Huns wear it.

In-Front-of-Grindir (*Fyrir Grindum*): **9**, a place where Helgi stations some of his troops.

Jarisleif (*Jarisleifr*), probably Jaroslav the Great of Russia (1015–1054): **34**, accompanies the sons of Gjuki on their journey to Denmark to be reconciled with Gudrun.

Jonakr (*Jónakr*): **32**, upon dying, Brynhild prophesies Gudrun's marriage to Jonakr; **41**, a king who marries Gudrun, by whom he has sons Hamdir, Sorli, and Erp; **42**, consents to Jormunrek's marriage to Svanhild.

Jormunrek (*Jörmunrekr*), Ermanaric, king of the Goths: **32**, upon dying, Brynhild prophesies Svanhild's marriage to Jormunrek; **42**, seeks Svanhild in marriage; believes Bikki's slander that she has had a love affair with his son Randver; has Randver hanged and Svanhild trampled to death by horses; **43**, Gudrun incites her sons to take revenge on Jormunrek for killing Svanhild; **44**, Hamdir and Sorli cut off his hands and feet; Jormunrek has Hamdir and Sorli stoned to death.

King of the Danes (*Danakonungr*): **31**, the sons of Gjuki killed the king of the Danes.

Kostbera (*Kostbera*) or Bera: **35**, Hogni's wife; deciphers the runes sent by Gudrun warning of Atli's treachery, even though they have been falsified by Vingi; [**36**, tells Hogni her dreams foreboding Atli's treachery]; **37**, bids Hogni farewell.

Laganess (*Láganess*), a place: **9**, Sinfjotli's insult to Granmar, "I sired nine wolves on you at Laganess."

Langobards (*Langbarðar*), a Germanic people: **34**, accompany the sons of Gjuki on their journey to Denmark to be reconciled with Gudrun.

Leif (*Leifr*): **9**, captain of Helgi's ship.

Loki (*Loki*), a supernatural trickster, companion and sometimes opponent of the gods: **14**, slays Otr; captures the dwarf Andvari and forces him to give up his gold so that the gods can pay it as compensation for Otr.

Lyngvi (*Lyngvi Hundingsson*): **11**, son of Hunding; rival suitor of Hjordis who makes war on Sigmund; **12**, is victorious in battle but fails to obtain Hjordis; **17**, killed by Sigurd.

Need (*Nauð*): **21**, a runic symbol marked on the fingernail to guard against poison.

Niflung (*Niflungr Högnason*): **40**, son of Hogni; helps Gudrun kill Atli.

Norns (*Nornir*), supernatural women who control the fates of men: **8**, prophesy Helgi's future fame at his birth; **14**, a Norn decreed that the dwarf Andvari should live in the water; **18**; the Norns separate sons from their mothers; some are of the race of Æsir, some are of the race of elves, and some are daughters of Dvalin; **21**, runes carved on a Norn's nail.

Norvasund (*Nörvasund*): **9**, a place from which a troop comes to join Helgi's forces.

Oddrun (*Oddrún*), Atli's sister: **32**, upon dying, Brynhild prophesies Gunnar's love affair with Oddrun.

Odin (*Óðinn*), foremost of the Norse gods: **1**, father of Sigi; gives his outlawed son warships and troops; sends his wish-maiden to childless Rerir with apple of fertility; **2**, Rerir dies, goes home to Odin; [**3**, thrusts sword into Barnstock]; [**8**, Odin's raven brings a leaf to heal Sinfjotli]; [**10**, takes Sinfjotli's body]; [**11**, breaks Sigmund's sword with his spear in the midst of a battle]; **12**, Sigmund says: "Odin does not want me to wield the sword since it is now broken"; **13**, advises Sigurd on how to choose a horse; **14**, forced by Hreidmar to pay Andvari's gold in compensation for Otr; attempts to hold for himself the cursed ring Andvaranaut, but is forced to relinquish it; **14**, Andvari's father; [**17**, hails Sigurd from a headland as Sigurd is sailing to avenge his father]; [**18**, advises Sigurd how to slay the dragon]; **21**, Odin promised victory to Hjalmgunnar, but Brynhild struck him down in battle; in revenge, Odin stuck Brynhild with a sleep-thorn, and said that she should never afterward have a victory and that she must marry; [**44**, advises that Hamdir and Sorli be stoned to death]. *See also* Feng, Fjolnir, Hnikar, Hropt.

Oin (*Óinn*): **14**, Andvari's father [the spelling Óðinn in the manuscript is almost certainly a mistake; *see* "The Lay of Regin"].

Orkning (*Orkningr*): **37**, a renowned champion; brother of Bera; accompanies his brother-in-law Hogni to Atli's stronghold.

Oskapt (*Óskaptr*): **18**, "the uncreated," an island where Surt and the Æsir will mix together their blood.

Otr (*Otr Hreiðmarsson*): **14**, son of Hreidmar; is accustomed to fish in the likeness of an otter; is killed by the gods while in the shape of an otter; his father demands that the gods stuff the otter skin and cover it with gold as compensation for Otr.

Ran (*Rán*), goddess of the sea: **14**, Loki borrows her net to catch the dwarf Andvari in the shape of a pike.

GLOSSARY

Randver (*Randvérr Jörmunreksson*): **42**, Jormunrek's son, slanderously accused by Bikki of having a love affair with Svanhild; Jormunrek has him hanged; he sends his father a plucked hawk, a
token that Jormunrek is plucking out his own honor, but Jormunrek receives the message too late to save Randver.

Raudabjorg (*Rauðabjörg*): **9**, the place where Helgi's troops meet.

Regin (*Reginn Hreiðmarsson*): **13**, son of Hreidmar; foster father
of Sigurd; urges Sigurd to slay Fafnir; **14**, tells Sigurd the story of
how Fafnir obtained the gold treasure and became a dragon; **15**,
forges sword Gram for Sigurd; **16** and **17**, urges Sigurd to slay Fafnir; **18**, takes Sigurd to slay Fafnir; **19**, drinks Fafnir's blood; in-
structs Sigurd to roast Fafnir's heart for him to eat; **20**, bird reveals
that Regin is plotting treachery against Sigurd; Sigurd slays Regin;
**25**, Brynhild weaves death of Regin into the tapestry of Sigurd's
deeds; **29**, Regin had owned Grani's harness; **31**, Sigurd praised for
killing Regin.

Rerir (*Rerir Sigason*): **1**, son of Sigi; kills his kin to avenge his
father; childless, receives apple of fertility from Odin's wish-
maiden; **2**, dies; goes home to Odin.

Rhine River (*Rín*): **26**, Gjuki's kingdom lies south of the Rhine; **30**,
Gudrun and Brynhild bathe in the Rhine, where they quarrel; **39**,
the Rhine shall have the gold before the Huns wear it.

Ridill (*Riðill*): **19**, a sword; Sigurd cuts out Fafnir's heart with it.

Rognir (*Rögnir*): **21**, runes were cut under Rognir's chariot.

Saxons (*Saxar*), a Germanic people: **34**, accompany the sons of
Gjuki on their journey to be reconciled with Gudrun.

Sigar (*Sigarr*): **26**, he took away with him one sister of Haki and
Hagbard and burned another in her house.

Sigar (*Sigarr*): **34**, Gudrun and Thora's tapestry shows battle of
Sigar and Siggeir in the south of Fjon.

Siggeir (*Siggeirr*): **3**, king of Gautland; marries Signy; fails to draw sword from Barnstock; **4**, treacherously invites Volsung and his sons to visit him; **5**, puts Volsung's sons in stocks to be killed by a she-wolf who is his mother; **6**, his sons killed by Sigmund; **8**, puts Sigmund and Sinfjotli alive in a mound; is burned in his house by Sigmund and Sinfjotli; **9**, insult directed at Sinfjotli: "You are the stepson of King Siggeir."

Siggeir (*Siggeirr*): **34**, Gudrun and Thora's tapestry shows the battle of Sigar and Siggeir in the south of Fjon.

Sigi (*Sigi Óðinsson*): **1**, son of Odin; outlawed for killing thrall Bredi; rules over Hunland; father of Rerir; killed by his wife's brother.

Sigmund (*Sigmundr Völsungsson*), king of Hunland: **2**, son of Volsung; **3**, draws sword from Barnstock; **5**, put in stocks by Siggeir to be killed by a she-wolf; escapes; **6**, tests and kills Signy's sons by Siggeir; **7**, mates with Signy, begetting Sinfjotli; tests Sinfjotli; **8**, lives in the forest in wolf shape; kills Siggeir; marries Borghild and fathers Helgi; **10**, his son Sinfjotli poisoned; **11**, marries Hjordis; is forced to do batttle with her other suitor Lyngvi; [Odin] breaks Sigmund's sword in the battle; **12**, tells Hjordis that she will bear his son Sigurd; dies from wounds; **15**, his broken sword given to Sigurd; **16**, Sigurd says that he must avenge Sigmund; **17**, his son Sigurd kills Lyngvi and Hjorvard in order to avenge him; **18, 21, 26, 28**, Sigurd identified as son of Sigmund; **32**, Brynhild had promised to marry the son of Sigmund; **34**, Gudrun weaves a tapestry showing ships of Sigmund.

Sigmund (*Sigmundr Sigurðarson*): **28**, son of Sigurd and Gudrun; [**32**, Brynhild urges that Sigurd's son be killed; the dying Sigurd fears that his son will be killed]; [**33**, Brynhild has had Sigurd's three-year-old son killed; he is burned on the pyre with Sigurd and Brynhild]; **34**, Gudrun's brothers compensate her for the death of her son; Grimhild urges Gudrun to let sons by Atli take the place of her son Sigmund.

Signy (*Signý Völsungsdóttir*): **2**, daughter of Volsung; **3**, married to Siggeir; **4**, foretells unhappiness for her family from Siggeir; **5**, tries to warn Volsung of Siggeir's treachery; contrives a plan to save Sigmund's life; **6**, sends her two sons by Siggeir to Sigmund for testing; **7**, mates with Sigmund, gives birth to Sinfjotli, sends him to Sigmund for testing; **8**, contrives Sigmund's and Sinfjotli's escape from the mound; chooses to die in burning house with Siggeir.

Sigrun (*Sigrún Högnadóttir*): **9**, a shield-maiden (i.e., a valkyrie), daughter of Hogni, who is betrothed against her will to Hodbrodd; she incites Helgi to kill Hodbrodd and marry her.

Sigurd (*Sigurðr Sigmundarson*): **13**, posthumous son of Sigmund; born to Hjordis; chooses horse Grani; urged by foster father Regin to slay Fafnir; **14**, Regin tells him the story of the origin of Fafnir's hoard; **15**, Regin forges sword Gram for him; **16**, his fate prophesied by Gripir; **17**, kills Lyngvi and Hjorvard to avenge his father Sigmund; **18**, slays dragon Fafnir; **19**, roasts Fafnir's heart; tastes Fafnir's blood; understands the speech of birds; **20**, learns of Regin's treachery from speech of birds; slays Regin; takes Fafnir's hoard; **21**, awakens Brynhild on Hindarfell; obtains runes from her; **22**, Brynhild gives him wise advice; he pledges to marry her; **23**, Sigurd described; **24**, visits Heimir; **25**, meets with Brynhild at Heimir's house; he pledges to marry her; gives her a gold ring; **26**, Brynhild and Gudrun are discussing famous men, and Brynhild praises Sigurd; **27**, Brynhild predicts Gudrun's marriage to Sigurd; **28**, goes to King Gjuki; is given a drink by Grimhild which makes him forget Brynhild; marries Gudrun; swears brotherhood with Gunnar and Hogni; **29**, rides through Brynhild's wall of flame in the guise of Gunnar, winning Brynhild as wife for Gunnar; **30**, Brynhild and Gudrun quarrel over the relative merits of Gunnar and Sigurd, and Gudrun reveals that it was Sigurd, not Gunnar, who rode through Brynhild's wall of flame; **31**, tries to placate angry Brynhild, reveals his love for her; **32**, killed by Guttorm at Brynhild's and Gunnar's instigation; **33**, Brynhild gives Gunnar instructions for Sigurd's funeral pyre, on which she too will be burned; **34**, Sigurd's renown praised; Gudrun laments Sigurd; **35**, Atli desires the gold hoard that Sigurd had owned; **38**, Atli demands of Gunnar the treasure of Sigurd; **40**, Gudrun laments: "Life was better when I was with Sigurd"; **41**, Sigurd and Gudrun have a daughter named Svanhild; **42,** Svanhild is daughter of Sigurd Fafnir's Bane; **43,** Gudrun longs to join Sigurd in death.

Sinfjotli (*Sinfjötli Sigmundarson*): **7,** son of Sigmund and Signy; passes test set by Sigmund; **8,** lives in the forest in wolf shape; is wounded and then cured when a raven brings a healing leaf to Sigmund; joins Sigmund in revenge against Siggeir; **9,** joins Helgi in expedition against Hodbrodd; engages in a *senna,* or contest of insults, with Granmar; **10,** poisoned by his stepmother Borghild.

Skadi (*Skaði*): **1,** owner of the thrall Bredi.

Sleipnir (*Sleipnir*), Odin's eight-legged horse: **13,** Sigurd's horse Grani is descended from Sleipnir; **21,** runes were cut on Sleipnir's reins.

Snaevar (*Snævarr Högnason*): **37,** son of Hogni; accompanies his father to Atli's stronghold.

Sok (*Sök*): **9,** an island near which Helgi stations part of his troops.

Solar (*Sólarr Högnason*): **37,** son of Hogni; accompanies his father to Atli's stronghold.

Solfell (*Sólfjöll*), an unidentified place: **8,** Sigmund's naming gift to Helgi; **9,** Granmar and Hodbrodd meet at Solfell.

Sorli (*Sörli Jónakrsson*): **41,** Gudrun's sons by Jonakr; **44,** kills Erp; cuts off Jormunrek's feet; is stoned to death.

Surt (*Surtr*), a fire-giant: **18,** Surt and the Æsir will mix together their blood on the island called Oskapt.

Svafrlod (*Svafrlöð*): **31,** a woman of the court who expresses concern and alarm over Brynhild's state of mind.

Svanhild (*Svanhildr Sigurðardóttir*): **32,** upon dying, Brynhild prophesies her marriage to Jormunrek and subsequent misfortune;

**41**, daughter of Sigurd and Gudrun; exceptionally beautiful, with keen eyes; **42**, married to Jormunrek; slanderously accused by Bikki of having a love affair with Randver; put to death by being trampled by horses; **43**, Gudrun incites her sons to avenge Svanhild.

Svarinshaug (*Svarinshaugr*): **9**, the region ruled by King Hodbrodd's brother, possibly the Schwerin district.

Sveggjud (*Sveggjuðr*): **9**, a horse belonging to Hodbrodd.

Sveipud (*Sveipuðr*): **9**, a horse belonging to Granmar.

Thora (*Þóra Hákonardóttir*): **34**, daughter of Hakon; Gudrun takes refuge in Denmark with Thora.

Thrasness (*Þrasnes*), a place: **9**, insult directed at Sinfjotli: "You were gelded by the giant's daughters on Thrasness."

Tyr (*Týr*), a god: **21**, invoke Tyr when writing war runes.

Vaerings (*Væringjar*), Scandinavians: **23**, reference to "the dragon called Fafnir by the Vaerings."

Valbjorg (*Valbjörg*): **34**, a place given to Gudrun as compensation for her husband and her son.

Valdamar of Denmark (*Valdamarr af Danmörk*): **34**, accompanies the sons of Gjuki on their journey to Denmark to be reconciled with Gudrun.

Valkyrie (*Valkyrja*): **9**, insult directed at Granmar: "You were a valkyrie in Asgard." *See also* Brynhild, Hljod, Sigrun.

Vanir (*Vanir*), a class of Norse gods largely concerned with fertility and prosperity: **21**, possess runes.

Varinsey (*Varinsey*), an unidentified island: **9**, insult directed at Granmar: "You were a witch on Varinsey."

Varinsfjord (*Varinsfjörðr*): **9**, unidentified fjord where a storm overtakes Helgi.

Vinbjorg (*Vínbjörg*): **34**, a place given to Gudrun as compensation for her husband and son.

Vingi (*Vingi*): **35**, Atli's messenger to Gunnar and Hogni; falsifies Gudrun's message warning of Atli's treachery; **37**, accompanies Gunnar and Hogni to Atli's stronghold; reveals his treachery and threatens to hang them; they beat him to death.

Volsung (*Völsungr Rerisson*): **2**, born by being cut from his mother's body; marries, has children, builds a hall; **3**, gives his daughter Signy in marriage to Siggeir; **4**, dismisses Signy's warning, accepts Siggeir's treacherous invitation; **5**, killed by Siggeir; **8**, mentioned; **21**, Sigurd identifies himself as being of the line of Volsung.

Volsungs (*Völsungar*), descendants of King Volsung: **6, 7, 8, 9, 10, 11, 12, 13, 17, 40.**

Wavering flames (*Vafrlogi*), Odin creates wall of flames around the sleeping Brynhild: [**21**, approaching Hindarfell, Sigurd sees a light, as if a fire were burning]; **29**, Sigurd in guise of Gunnar rides through Brynhild's wall of flame; **30**, Gudrun reveals that it was Sigurd, not Gunnar, who rode through her wavering flames.

Designer: Donna L. Wittlin
Compositor: Prestige Typography
Text: 10/12 Sabon
Display: Sabon
Printer: Maple-Vail Book Manufacturing Group
Binder: Maple-Vail Book Manufacturing Group